Introduction to Social Research

With Applications
to the Caribbean

Ian Boxill

Claudia Chambers

Eleanor Wint

Canoe Press University of the West Indies

Barbados ● Jamaica ● Trinidad and Tobago

I0112389

Canoe Press University of the West Indies
1A Aqueduct Flats   Mona
Kingston 7 Jamaica

ISBN 976-8125-22-5

06   5 4

CATALOGUING IN PUBLICATION DATA

Boxill, Ian
   Introduction to social research : with Applications to the
   Caribbean / Ian Boxill, Claudia Chambers, Eleanor Wint

   p. cm.

   ISBN 976-8125-22-5

   1. Social sciences – Research – Caribbean, English-speaking.
   I. Chambers, Claudia. II. Wint, Eleanor. III. Title

   H62.B686 1997   300.7 dc-20

Set in Stone Informal 10/14pt, with Stone Sans display
Book design by Prodesign Limited
Cover design by Vernon Films

Photographs: Chapter 1, 3, 4, 6-11 Courtesy of the Public Relations Office, UWI Mona
Chapter 2 Courtesy of the Librarian, UWI Mona
Chapter 5 Courtesy of the Campus Registrar and the Director, Caribbean Institute of
Media and Communications, UWI Mona

*Time makes us forget many deeds
and those responsible for their implementation.*

*The authors of this book wish to dedicate the publication to the memories of
the late Dr Derek Gordon and the late Professor Carl Stone, both of whom were
leading scholars, researchers and teachers in the Faculty of Social Sciences,
University of the West Indies, Mona, Jamaica. Their works will undoubtedly
always exist as a foundation for the Caribbean's new breed of researcher.*

CONTENTS

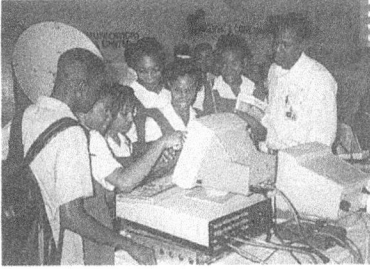

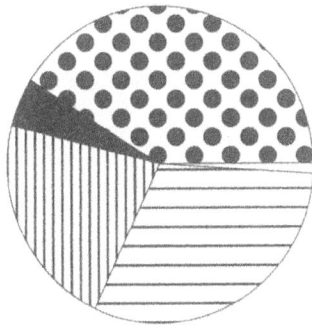

List of Figures, Tables, and Text Boxes

Figures

Tables

Text Boxes

Preface

This book aims to provide its readers with an introduction to social research, with special emphasis on the Caribbean. At present there are very few texts on social research with a Caribbean focus, the most popular ones reflecting experiences in North America and the United Kingdom. Therefore, our motivation for writing this book was to provide students with a fairly comprehensive guide to the fundamentals of social research, drawing on the experiences of the Caribbean. In that regard the work represents a pioneering effort.

While this publication is perhaps the most comprehensive research text on the elements of social research methods with a Caribbean focus, it follows in a long line of writings on aspects of social research by Caribbean social scientists such as the late Carl Stone and the late Derek Gordon. This publication has drawn on both the inspiration and ideas of some of the works in that line.

This book is divided into eleven chapters. The first two chapters deal with the research process and conceptual issues in social research. Chapters three and four discuss the structure of the inquiry process. In chapters five to nine we highlight different methods of observation, broadly divided into obtrusive and unobtrusive techniques. Chapter ten is concerned with techniques for analysing and presenting data, while chapter eleven looks at ethical and political issues in social research.

We could not have completed this publication without the assistance of numerous individuals. We would like to thank Professor Frank Santopolo of Colorado State University for allowing us to reproduce a number of his writings on social research. We are grateful to our many students at the University of the West Indies, who provided the stimulus for this publication. In addition, we would like to acknowledge the assistance and professional guidance of members of The Press UWI – particularly Pansy Benn, Linda Cameron, Shivaun Hearne, Taitu Heron and Marjorie Moyston. For assistance with typing we thank Annika Lewison. It is our hope that the tremendous efforts combined in this work will be fruitful over the longer term.

I. Boxill
C. Chambers
E. Wint

Chapter One

What Is Social Research?

When astronomers looked at the sun, they saw it as an orb circling the earth. When the Copernican system arose as an alternative to this view, it offered little empirical data. Instead, it described the "old facts" in a different way. A shift of vision was required for people to see the sun as star, not a planet of the earth. [Mehan and Wood 1994: 316.]

Introduction

Human beings are naturally curious. From the time that we are born we are curious about our environment. We constantly seek to understand various phenomena around us. This book seeks to provide skills to help in understanding what we see around us. Here we are concerned with the social world.

All of us have ways of knowing things, but they are not all equal. For instance, how many times have you heard someone make a generalization from a personal experience or observation? When last were you in a discussion in which someone made a statement similar to: Cricket is popular among Barbadians because all of the Barbadians I know play cricket? Now while cricket may, in fact, be popular in Barbados, there is no way that we can prove that cricket is popular among Barbadians simply on the basis of this anecdotal evidence.

We also know things through what Babbie [1992] calls "agreement reality". That is, things that are considered to be true because they are what other people accept to be true. Suppose you have been hearing for many years that cricket is not a popular sport among Barbadians, you may conclude that those Barbadians who play the game are really exceptions within the society. In this case your understanding of cricket in Barbados is based on your agreement with what other people say rather than your own observation. Again, it is impossible to judge the veracity of that conclusion simply on the basis of what other people say.

Which begs the question: How do we determine what is true and what is not? This book aims to provide you with one such way, the scientific method. This method incorporates aspects of personal observation and 'agreement reality' but in a way that allows us to test our conclusions. Especially for you the less experienced researcher, the scientific method requires a 'shift in vision', away from the intuitive, casual observation to a more empirical based, systematic approach (Table 1.1). However, before we discuss the scientific method in more detail, let us briefly look at two other ways of acquiring knowledge.

Table 1.1 Characteristics of scientific and non-scientific approaches to knowledge

	Non-scientific	Scientific
General approach:	Intuitive	Empirical
Observation:	Casual, uncontrolled	Systematic
Reporting:	Biased, subjective	Unbiased, objective
Concepts:	Ambiguous	Clear definitions
Instruments:	Inaccurate, imprecise	Accurate, precise
Measurement:	Not valid or reliable	Valid and reliable
Hypotheses:	Untestable	Testable
Attitude:	Uncritical, accepting	Critical, skeptical

Source: John J. Shaughnessy and Eugene B. Zechmeister. *Research Methods in Psychology*. New York: McGraw-Hill, 1994, p. 7

Knowledge by tradition

Many of us might be able to recall the many home-grown remedies given to us by parents or grandparents to cure a variety of illnesses. In some parts of the Caribbean traditional remedies are thought to be superior to modern, technologically driven medicine. The knowledge to make traditional medicines derives from people's accumulated experiences and is passed down from generation to generation as part of the culture.

Other forms of traditional knowledge which have been passed down through generations in the Caribbean include information about the timing and effects of hurricanes, changes in the weather and where to go fishing. Traditional knowledge can be derived from oral tales, songs, poetry, school, peers and the family.

However, traditional knowledge has its weaknesses. Because traditional knowledge is inherently conservative, it discourages alternative perspectives or explanations. For instance, health workers in some Caribbean countries have found it difficult to change unsafe sexual practices because of traditional views about sex.

Knowledge by authority

The other important source of knowledge in the Caribbean is by way of persons or institutions considered to be experts or authorities on the matter. For instance, we are more likely to trust the views of a mechanic than a physician if we seek information on an automobile related problem. Likewise if we have a medical problem, we are more likely to listen to a physician rather than the mechanic.

Knowledge based on authority may be derived from many sources, ranging from the sports commentator to a religious organization which uses the Holy Bible or Koran. Knowledge gained by the use of authority figures, however, frequently finds the authority figure gaining more importance than the knowledge itself. In other words, the politician, herself, may become more important than the message she bears. Thereafter, all that she says is right, true and just, simply because she says so.

Scientific Research

We now return to our discussion on the scientific method. Scientific research is research that employs the scientific method or the systematic collection and analysis of information. More specifically, it assumes, first of all, that the researcher has maintained an atmosphere of scepticism and objectivity as part of the process of collecting information. Indeed, the major characteristic of the scientific method is the maintenance by the researcher of a position of impartiality and disinterestedness as he or she tries to remain free of pet theories and bias.

This atmosphere of scepticism and disinterestedness means that despite the evidence presented he or she is still open to possible alternative explanations. It means, therefore, that where findings appear to be inconsistent with expectations, to the scientific enquirer, the route is one of testing and retesting in an attempt to improve our concept of reality. As we build on concepts, it becomes clear that reasoning consists of three types: deductive reasoning, inductive reasoning and the combined inductive-deductive approach.

Thus if we build on specific observations, theorizing outwards from the particular to the general, following a specified logic and sequence, the reasoning is inductive. In sociological pursuits the reasoning is more often deductive, moving from grand theories to the particular. We are very familiar with international funding agencies encouraging sociological analyses of such issues as urban poverty or microenterprise, the assumption being that more effective programmes can then be initiated at the family and community levels. This is the deductive approach, the logic and sequence being governed by the choice of factors measured.

The combined inductive-deductive approach, however, is the approach most frequently utilized in modern scientific method by scientists. It is a combination that allows systematic observation and theorizing to triumph over authority and inadequate observations. Indeed, it is the most useful and effective approach as we progress toward valid, reliable, empirical science.

Scientific research, as a third way of knowing, has had a critical role to play in the socio-economic development of the Caribbean. For example, scientific research, as opposed to commonsense reasoning or reasoning by authority, tells policy makers what are the factors that cause poverty. Historians and economists alike have come to realize the value of empirical analysis as we attempt to move away from theories based on emotionally clouded analyses to scientific analysis.

An interesting observation which should be made as part of this introduction to the world of social research is that regardless of the method used to know and understand, what we seek to achieve are acceptable explanations of relationships between identified concepts, relationships which present themselves as behaviours, preferences, opinions of human subjects. The relationships can be between such factors as level of education attained and socio-economic status, or tendency to use praise and reward systems of discipline and knowledge of stages of psycho-social development. These explanations must then be tested, re-tested, analysed and fed back into life's experiences, as the human being is both subject and object of the study.

Just one caveat before we proceed: we are not claiming that the scientific method is necessarily the best method of obtaining knowledge in all instances. But since this book is about developing an understanding of the scientific method we emphasize its strengths over its limitations.

Types of Relationships

Relationships are usually presented as statements. These statements can be termed assumptions or propositions. They are really the first attempt by the researcher to clarify for both self and reader, the major concepts which are under consideration, broadly defining in easily acceptable terms their relationship to each other.

If we look at the figure representing the research process (Figure 1.1), we will see that the process of preliminary formulation of an assumption or proposition falls in the top half of the figure. At this stage the researcher is still formulating or conceptualizing the type of relationship to be studied and has not yet reached to the formulation of a hypothesis. An analytical proposition or assumption suggests there is a substantial amount of formative work yet to be done before the researcher can begin to think about cause or association.

Causal relationships

A causal relationship is one in which some presumed factor (or series of factors) is thought to determine another factor (or series of factors). Let us take the following example of an analytical proposition looking at worker satisfaction – the level of education attained is most likely to be the key factor in determining the level of satisfaction experienced on the job. As an analytical proposition it proposes that *the level of education attained by the worker has a direct influence on*

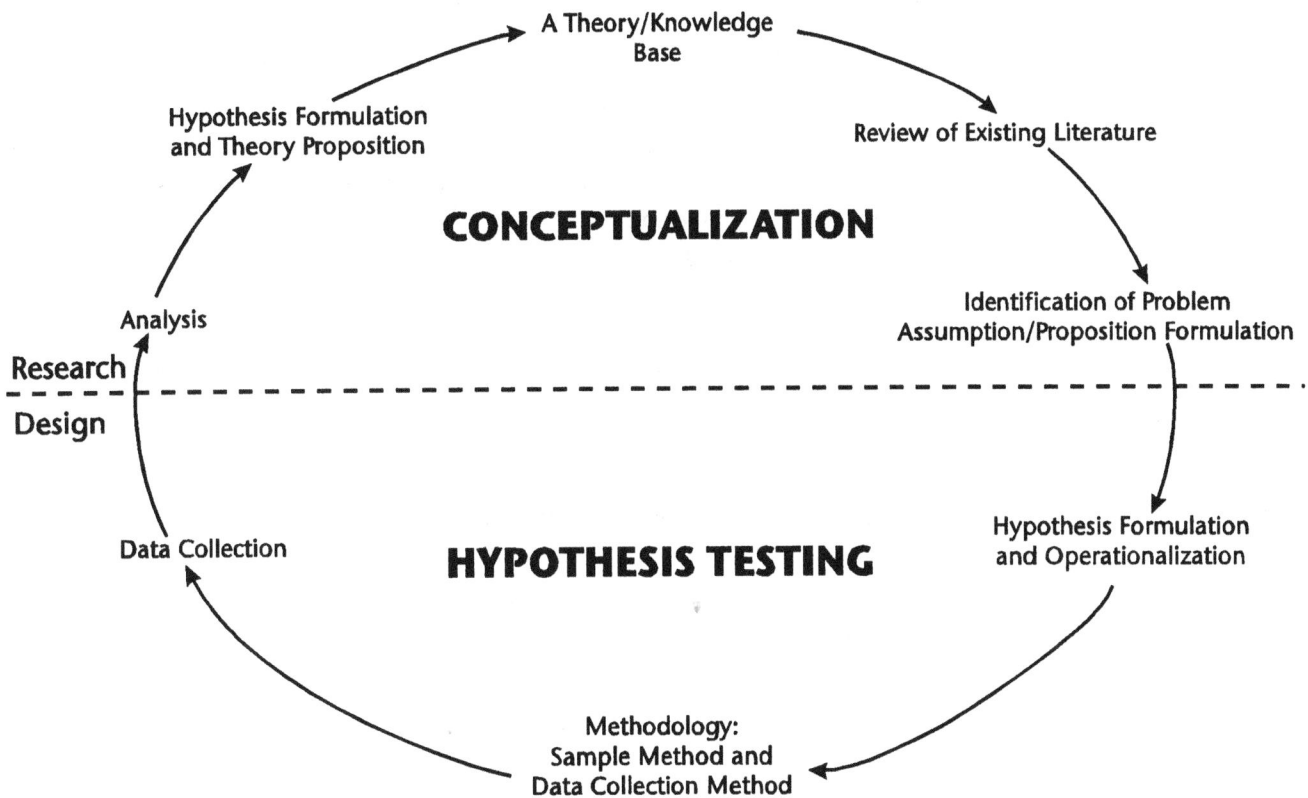

Figure 1.1   The Research Process

whether the worker feels satisfied or dissatisfied with her/his job. If we wish to move the proposition into a statement of cause, then the statement becomes *the level of satisfaction experienced on the job is directly dependent on the level of education attained by the worker.* This is now a causal relationship as it proposes that level of education attained is the critical factor determining job satisfaction.

Associational relationships

In this instance a change in either the direction or magnitude of one factor will be accompanied by a change in either direction or magnitude of another factor. If we take the example above, the associational proposition would posit that: level of education attained is directly or indirectly related to quality of job satisfaction. This is the type of statement one is more accustomed to and indeed the type of relationship proposition which we encourage you, the beginner, to make at this stage. Cause is so difficult to address in scientific research that perhaps it is best that we stay away from such statements at this stage.

Think about it. If we are to attribute job satisfaction solely to the level of education, then all other possible explanations/factors should be accounted for, or as we say in research, controlled for. Thus, for example, one would have to be sure that job satisfaction was not influenced also by, say, position held or salary offered. To control for other factors is very difficult simply because we are working with human subjects. Our behaviours, preferences, attitudes change from day to day and are not as easily controlled as drops of sulphuric acid.

The associational relationship does not attribute cause but rather points to particular factors which have a significant role in the eventual outcome. Positing that level of education attained is directly related to quality of job satisfaction opens up numerous possibilities for testing. More directly stated, this type of proposition can be termed a correlational relationship if we include some statement of magnitude and direction of association. For example: workers who have attained a tertiary level of education will exhibit a higher level of job satisfaction than those without a tertiary level of education.

Main Points

- Human beings are naturally curious. We constantly seek to understand the world around us.

- There are scientific and non-scientific (viz. tradition and authority) ways of acquiring knowledge about things around us.

- Both tradition and authority are valid ways of obtaining knowledge, and are often used along with the scientific approach to help us understand social reality.

- Non-scientific approaches to knowledge are limited by the fact that the hypotheses are untested; measurements are weak on validity and reliability; observation is casual and uncontrolled; concepts are ambiguous; and the attitude of the observer tends to be uncritical.

- The scientific method/approach to knowledge uses empirical evidence based on systematic observation, with clear definitions of concepts, valid and reliable measurement, testable hypotheses and an attitude of scepticism.

- The scientific method employs three major ways of reasoning: inductive, deductive and the combined inductive-deductive.

- There are two types of relationships: causal and associational. A causal relationship is one in which one variable is thought to determine the variation in another. An association relationship is one in which two variables vary together.

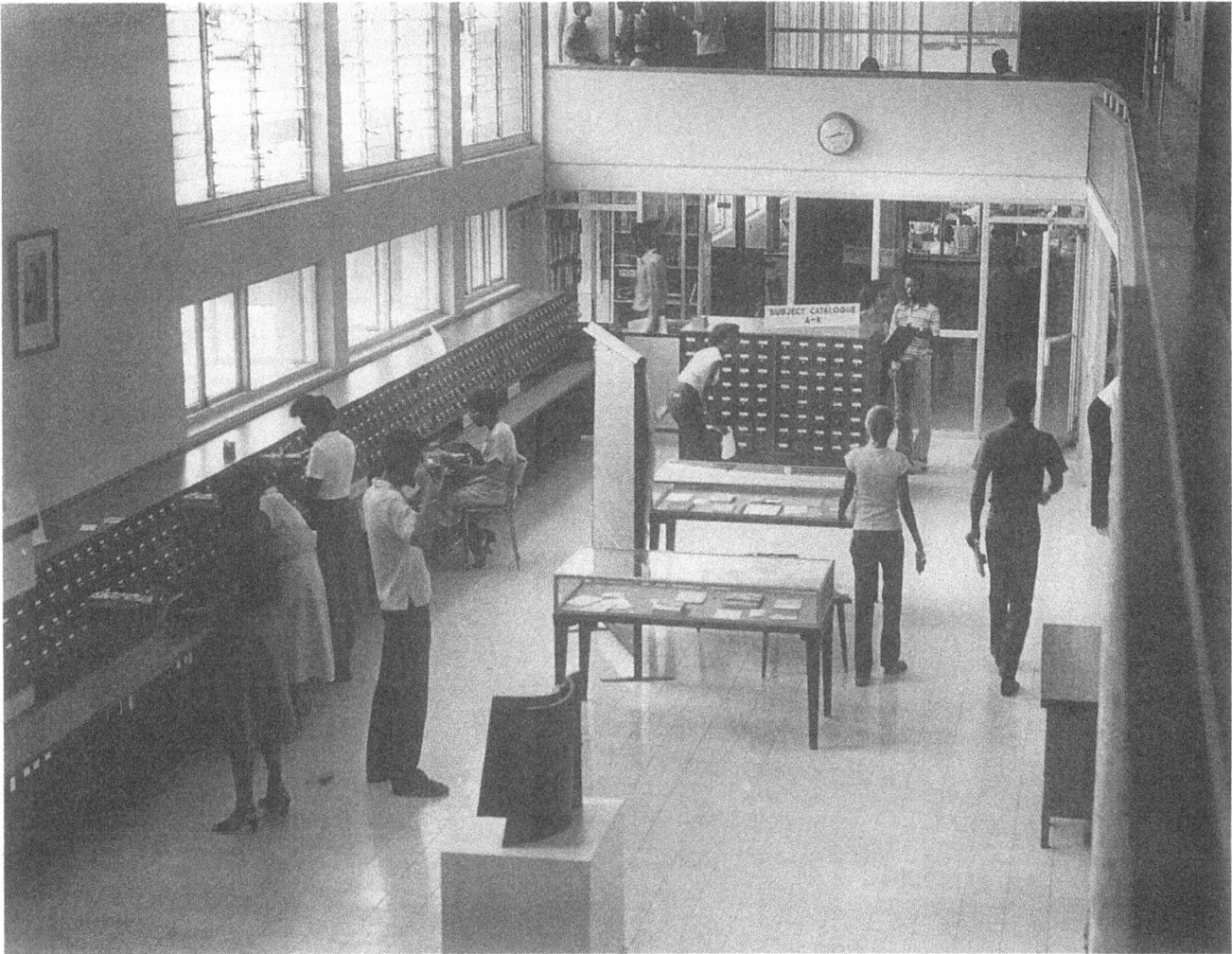

Chapter Two

Research and Theory

A writer once said: "Much modern social theory is either unintelligible, or banal or pointless . . . Few people feel at home with theory or use it in a productive way" [Craib 1984: 3]. Although most people feel uncomfortable thinking about theory, understanding it is not so difficult after all. We need theories as a part of good research. Theory helps us to explain social reality in a coherent and logical way.

We cannot settle debates on value, or what is moral, or what is 'best' for the population by the simplistic application of theories. What we can do is to report on substantive differences between groups of persons, attempting to distinguish the significant and predictive factors. Reports which address the tendency for particular violent crimes to be predominant in different geographical zones or the appearance of domestic violence across all socio-economic groups, allow researchers to develop theories which are then testable in similar circumstances.

We should keep in mind that a theory is no more than "a generalized, synthetic, explanatory statement" [Lastricci 1963], that interrelates a set of more specific propositions.

Theories are general, applying to more than one situation, synthetic in that they are devised abstractions and frequently can also be devised explanations. In this way a theory will provide satisfactory answers to all the questions the scientists know to ask. Theories do not provide all the answers, but specific answers, that is, those questions that we ask. As a systematic explanation for the observed facts and laws that relate to a particular aspect of life, a theory identifies the relevant factors, their relationships and their meanings.

Use of Theories

How do we know which theory to apply? Take the earlier example of the relationship between violent crimes and geographic and social location. First the researcher might well have to answer the following questions: What is your view of your surrounding social world? What is your understanding of how people behave? What is your knowledge of criminal activity? What is the reason behind the research question/concern? Answering these questions would allow the researcher to appreciate and state his or her preference for a particular way of understanding and searching for explanations for this phenomenon and therefore to adopt a particular theoretical stance. The statement of his or her preference should be made at the outset of the research, as it will guide methodological and analytical procedures throughout the research and consequently guide the reader's understanding.

The Parts of a Theory

Concepts

Concepts are the building blocks of a theory. A concept is a generalized idea about an entire class of objective phenomena. A concept really represents an idea we have about something observed. It is expressed as a symbol. Most frequently this symbol is a word. Words are also symbols, so when we use words frequently we are talking about concepts. For example, how is 'cake' a concept? The word cake has been given a very general meaning by society usually referring to some kind of baked goods, probably made up of flour, eggs, milk and so on.

If we wanted to be less specific and more general, the concept could refer to a whole collection of tangible objects. In this instance it might be 'baked products'. A concept can also refer to an idea or an abstraction, something which does not exist in our sense experience.

If I asked you to give me an example of a dog, you might say Spot, or Brownie or Rex. Or you might say something you like to touch, bathe or walk. Altogether as dog, however, these only become concrete when we are specific and the features are identified. In slang we find that the concept 'dog' is an idea, hence we can nastily declare 'you are a dog'. More often than not in social science we encounter concepts which are more abstract; for example, terms such as socio-economic status, social control, cognitive dissonance. These concepts are usually given precise definitions so as to ease communication.

Concepts are usually words, (for example, table, occupation, education) but each word is an idea about a concrete object. To have meaning they have to be defined. So it would seem that a concept has two parts, viz. a symbol and a definition. We can learn concepts in everyday ways or in formal ways. Usually when we learn from everyday experiences, definitional concepts tend to be bound up with language and culture. The broad concept of socio-economic status is a definition inexorably bound up in culture. Not only will the social and economic indicators vary from culture to culture but so will the relative importance of the concept itself within the larger society. To try and create universal indicators is particularly challenging. Derek Gordon [1989] was noted for his development of a poverty line based on the *Survey of Living Conditions, Jamaica* as a yearly indicator useful for policy analysts, nutrition specialists, child-rearing strategies and the interpretation of international human/social indicators.

Striving for explanation and acceptance social scientists continue to be concerned with giving concepts scientific definitions which should facilitate a more universal understanding. The real problem with which we are faced however is that of jargon and the specificity of terms within disciplines.

Constructs

A construct is a generalized idea about an entire class of subjective phenomena. Both concepts and constructs are general, both are ideas and refer to classes of things. The important difference to remember is that the construct refers to intangible phenomena, for example, love. The construct 'love' may be defined as an intangible feeling with an affective component. Since very few researchers distinguish between concepts and constructs we will use the word concept to refer to both terms.

Concepts and theory

When we began discussing parts of a theory, the first statement described concepts as the building block of a theory. Having discussed this, it should now be clear that it is important for the researcher to build theory on facts and not whims. Although many theories that we encounter in the social sciences are developed after observation of one or two selected cases or events, the critical encounter has allowed the researcher to employ a systematic method of observation over an extended period of time. The researcher has been able to move a vague concept to something measurable in the empirical world.

We need to understand research as utilizing theory first of all as a conceptual tool, relating concepts in a particular model. This allows the researcher to become aware of possible relationships which can be studied and introduces the critical constructs or concepts which need to be addressed. Having done that, the researcher, on completion of the empirical exercise, is able to analyse or interpret findings within a particular framework thus leading to recommendations for action (applied research) or new conceptual theories (basic research). A precise understanding of the concepts encountered in the theory is necessary if the research is to lead to either logical abstraction or empirical reasoning.

Two Views of the Social World

As we move from the conceptual to the analytic stage, the decisions on methodology will be guided by the assumptions of social reality held by the researcher. To assume that all around is concrete, directly measurable and clearly objective (the positivist approach) is an opposing view to that which views the world as soft, personal and yielding. Some writers term these views the positivist or the objectivist approach and the anti-positivist or the subjectivist approach.

If we prefer the positivist approach, which sees the social world as hard, objective reality, then the methodology which will be used for data collection is quantitative, that is, reducing data to and relying on numerical representations. Consider the problem of accessing skills training. Perhaps the social scientist is concerned with the poor turnout of women at the skills training centre and posits that this is attributable to a gender preference. The question with which she or he might be faced is: Is there a grand theory? If we try to apply a grand theory we might use the example of the relationship between gender and access to skills training. The question would then be, do social interpretations of gender in the Caribbean inhibit free access to traditional and non-traditional skills-training? A quantitative approach would be concerned with examining the relationships between the factors in question and seeing how best the generalizable, universal laws explain those relationships. The qualitative approach on the other hand would prefer to emphasize the individual experience of a specific set of women perhaps, representing new interpretations from each gender perspective. Hence, the question might then well be: Have women who have been attending skills-training centres noticed any new or increased tension between themselves and their male partners?

Across the social sciences, it is clear that the perspective with which we approach the study will influence not only the theoretical stance which is adopted but will also affect the methodological approach selected. Social science research spans many disciplines, with emphasis on the social world and human relationships. The two views of the social world allow the social scientist the added capacity to understand and interpret this challenging and changing environment in which we live.

Theory and Research

One of the criticisms made against the positivist school is that there is too much emphasis on objectivity. The criticism of the positivist school suggests that the social scientist needs to acknowledge more realistically the value of subjective knowing particularly when attempting to explain people's behaviours. Life is not as 'cut and dried' as we might wish to think and behaviours are influenced by both latent and manifest factors.

Subjective analysis such as is often employed in the social work profession has benefited greatly from an understanding of the 'peculiarity' of the individual realizing that an important aspect of data gathering is initial relationship building.

Work done in the field of group therapy and group dynamics by such authors as Homans and Bogardus would certainly not have progressed if a purely objective stance had been adopted. Social work as a profession, on the other hand, has in fact been able to use 'relationship' in a therapeutic mode, creating new insights into personality functioning [Hollis 1964, Wint 1991].

Both conceptual stances have nevertheless realized the need for theory whether as a generalizable framework (deductive reasoning) or springing from the individual experiences. Often we encounter social research which seems to be 'one-off', simply recounting in a descriptive manner the activities or progress of an event or a project. In reality, however, although seemingly unrelated, in many instances it is this contact between abstract theoretical considerations and empirical data gathering that leads to well-formulated applications. We cannot implement a programme without knowing for whom, under what constraints and why. Each of these assume not only a cultural and experiential familiarity with the clientele but includes also some understanding of the wider socio-economic and psychological theories which govern their behaviour.

Theory influences research and as Figure 1.1 on page 5 demonstrates, research output influences theory. At times the language of theories can seem strange, and even impossible to understand. We can all recall the mystique of those grand theories of stratification, anomie and so on in our first encounter with sociology.

The middle road seems the best road especially when starting out in social research. We need to aim for clarity, a particular ease of communication and a mix of abstraction and empiricism. Thinking about what you have learnt about how society functions can allow you, the student, to explain in your own words, say, Parsons' or Herskovits' concepts of society and then to apply this to a study which will build on observations of families, families in communities and communities as a whole.

In finding the mix, both the criteria of experience and a somewhat subjective problem solving or heuristic approach will have been combined with a healthy regard for some universality or commonness of life's experiences.

Scientific Method and the Research Process

In the scientific method we consider process and objectivity, order and method as we proceed to make researchable statements about a concept. The key assumptions underlying this process are objectivity, logical reasoning and systematic procedures.

As Figure 1.1 points out, theory is essential in beginning the classical research process. This theory uses the language of conceptualization, employing broad terms which are familiar to the particular discipline. The assumptions and propositions which flow from this theory employ a similar language moving the theory nearer to the operational stage. Thus we move from the process of theory and concept formulation to assumptions and propositions as the beginning stage of conceptualization.

In order to move to the next stage of the research process, that is hypothesis formulation and data collection, the language of operationalization must now be employed. Whereas objectivity and logical reasoning may have been the driving forces behind the process of conceptualization, order and systematic procedures now take over as the researcher seeks to find a methodology which will allow clarification of concepts in clear measurable terms.

Moving from conceptualization to operationalization is not an easy task as not all constructs or concepts lend themselves to easy operationalization. For example, satisfaction with campus life, poverty alleviation, financial management and mental retardation are all familiar concepts but each one presents significantly different challenges for operationalization.

The researcher, therefore, needs to bear in mind two important elements which will facilitate the transition from conceptualization to operationalization. These are clarity of perceptions and ease of objective observation.

Let us return to Figure 1.1

The researcher can begin from either of the extreme positions: 1) he or she knows very little about the particular subject; or 2) he or she has a theory which provides the answers to all the questions she or he needs to ask.

More frequently we are somewhere in between. However, in order to begin the research process and the conceptualization of the problem, recognition of an existing knowledge base is critically important. Let us say that there is a peculiar lack of information on the topic in question, then the researcher is faced with casting around for insights from a range of observations or experiences. But then, what are we supposed to observe: everything, anything? It is clear that we could end up with a wealth of information which is incoherent, no doubt interesting and probably non-generalizable. It would seem that where the researcher has failed to develop a theory or a conceptual model which can be used to identify the important concepts or constructs the transition to operationalization is fraught with pitfalls.

At the other extreme we might be aware of a theory which simply needs to be tested under new conditions. The researcher, however, might be so confident about the usefulness of the particular model that the uniqueness of the particular study may be by-passed in an attempt at conformity.

Clarity of perception and ease of objective observation, the two key elements in the process should be employed in both of these extreme positions. Scattered and accidental observations need to be replaced with structured and logical observations, observations which show a clear relationship to the perceived concepts. Similarly with broadbased theories, the researcher needs to realize the specificity of the study and the need for operationalizations which truly fit the case.

If the researcher is able to transform the concepts into unambiguous relationships, it means that she or he is now quite clear about the statement of the problem.

How to Zero In on a Problem

In order to study a problem or a question, we need first of all to have a good grasp of the kinds of research that exist on the problem or question. Of course, we will not know all that there is about the issue. That is impossible. But we should at least show some appreciation of what has gone before. To keep in mind the maxim, 'there is nothing new under the sun', is a sobering thought and good guidance.

Identification of the problem

Of course, the process is one of reading and filtering. As we read what has gone before, and talk to knowledgeable persons about our ideas, we get closer to identifying where our interest really lies. There is a gradual narrowing of the subject area to a specific research question or questions. If we are unable to frame our interest in the form of a question, we probably need to do more reading. It is useful to read, note, read, discuss, note, read again and then try and take a position. This gives us the opportunity to begin formulating and discarding research questions as we look for the one which best reflects both interest and research access. As we do this, reading, discussion and language become focused.

It is, however, not enough to say what your research problem is; social researchers also have to explain why a particular research problem is important. There are several motivating factors for research. These include:

- testing theory
- using theories to understand a research question
- challenging poor research
- clarifying an underlying process
- attempting to account for unexpected findings
- replication
- seeing if research in one area extends to another

The actual formulation of the question is governed by such thoughts as: Is the projected study worthwhile? What will it accomplish? Will it be used by policy makers or significantly contribute to the process of theory building? Whom will it serve? Is it feasible? Do we have the time and financial resources to accomplish the stated goal? Are subjects available? Will subjects cooperate? Are facilities/equipment available? Is it ethical? Do we overstep the ethical boundaries of personal dignity and perhaps put subjects in potential danger?

If we are able to satisfactorily answer these questions, we then find a new challenge, that is, where do we look for information which will guide our transition from conceptualization and question formulation to the next stage of operationalization?

Today researchers are faced with a plethora of information avenues. Here in the Caribbean the number of new libraries, research institutes and centres is increasing. Some of these are quite specialized like the Caribbean Centre for Development Administration and the Caribbean Food and Nutrition Institute while others cover a range of topics. Of course, the advent of surfing on the Internet has not passed us by, with territories boasting their own communication networks. Internet services are available in Barbados, Cayman, St Lucia, Jamaica, and Trinidad and Tobago, among others.

We also have recourse to

- professional journals (periodicals)
- monographs
- official government publications
- Caribbean-based data systems
- special information systems
- computerized information referral system
- books
- case files, life histories, newspapers
- audio-visual documentaries and files

The sources are endless.

Research Design

Let us again return to Figure 1.1

You will notice the dotted line representing the research design. Whenever a researcher engages in research there is always a preliminary planning stage. This is the stage which Babbie [1992: 89] terms designing a strategy for finding out something.

Research design cuts into the research process chart describing an artificial distinction between the thinking (conceptualization) and the doing (methodology and analysis).

In order to determine what type of research design is most useful for the investigation of a particular research problem, it is important to identify the purpose of the research. Thinking of a design forces the researcher to move into the realm of methodology. New questions which arise include such things as: With whom will I speak? What do I want to observe? Am I going to need a large number of agencies or persons or will a few do?

The researcher also makes the decision as to the use to which the study will be put; a decision which will directly influence the design preference – namely whether it will be exploratory, descriptive/formative or explanatory/predictive. Let us look at these preferences.

Exploratory studies are normally associated with topics that are relatively new and unstudied. For instance, suppose you observed that students in your tutorial group who were given As for course work in Social Research were predominantly from the Faculty of Education. This is worth more systematic exploration before drawing conclusions about the ability of students according to faculty. First, you might want to know the extent to which your observations are true for other tutorial groups, is the breakdown of grades similar, or do you find other faculties sharing the honours? It could be that your tutorial simply has more students from the Faculty of Education than any other faculty. Or perhaps you might wish to observe other features of the student body which you feel could have influenced grade allocation, such as age of student, previous experience in research, year of entry into their programme.

As we get involved in this investigation we arrive at a better understanding of the phenomenon under question. Exploratory studies usually suggest that the researcher needs to go through a process of understanding more fully the wider range of associational factors. It suggests also that the parameters of the population in question are not well known and the hope is that these kinds of issues will become clearer, probably leading to more definitive data gathering.

According to Babbie [1992: 90] there are three main reasons why people do exploratory studies: "(1) to satisfy the researcher's curiosity and desire for better understanding, (2) to test the feasibility of undertaking a more careful study, and (3) to develop the methods to be employed in a more careful study".

If we keep this in mind it becomes clear that the questions of sampling and method of data collection, both areas under that Research Design line in Figure 1.1, are not as critical as in other designs.

Next is the descriptive design. Here we take a step up the ladder in terms of attention to detail, greater stringency being employed in questionnaire design and sampling methodology. The descriptive design is, as the term implies, concerned with description. The intensity of the description, however, can vary.

Descriptive studies tell us what is happening in regard to the phenomenon being studied. For instance, the population census conducted every decade tells us what is happening to the demographic trends of a particular society. The kinds of questions that can be answered from the data include: Are there more women than men in the society? Are men and women having children earlier? Is the population growth rate increasing or is it declining? Are our people emigrating at a greater rate than before? It should be emphasized that descriptive studies do not tell us why the phenomena we observe exist. They serve rather to detail the phenomena and bring together descriptive indices in a way that can lead to a broadening of the theoretical focus.

With the explanatory design we attempt to "explain a social phenomenon by specifying why or how it happened" [Bailey 1989: 38]. The explanatory design employs more formal and scientific techniques of data collection. There is more attention to data collection methods, more attention paid to the strictness of the sampling design and, overall, an attempt to more strictly observe the rules of the scientific method. Whereas the descriptive/formative design may deal with associational relationships, explanatory studies tend toward causal explanations, seeking to find indicators which are able to predict and directly affect outcomes. Also, unlike the descriptive design, hypothesis formulation is *critical* to the process.

Let us take the example of a researcher's interest in the relationship between the incidence of late pregnancies and quality of family life. A descriptive design would probably be concerned with creating contrasting profiles of families in which parents had borne children at an older age as against those who had children at an earlier age. These profiles would describe in detail those characteristics or indicators which the researcher felt were important to understanding the relationship.

Were the same interest approached via the explanatory design, the researcher would postulate a direct associational or causal relationship between quality of family life and period at which parents chose to have their children. As was pointed out in the previous chapter, the causal relationship goes beyond description to suggest within certain limits, reasons for the behaviour of the phenomenon observed.

Some researchers make a distinction between studies that explain and those that predict. Others see them as basically the same. Although we do not want to enter into this debate, it is important to note that prediction presumes explanation, hence any attempt to predict must by definition involve some explanation.

Choosing a research design

There are many factors which influence a research design, one of which is time. We can make our observations at one point in time or stretch them out over a long period.

Cross-sectional studies are aimed at studying phenomena at a given time. Examples of this type of design include a Stone poll taken at a single interval, or a population census.

Cross-sectional studies are often exploratory or descriptive, but they can also be explanatory. The problem with cross-sectional studies is that they make conclusions about events which occur over time based on observations made at a single time period. We cannot say that the findings from a survey on the Jamaican political culture in 1995 will be the same ten years later.

Cross-sectional studies are particularly useful for providing snapshots, indepth descriptions which can stand alone, and projections on a range of indicators.

Longitudinal studies permit observations over an extended time period. In other words, multiple observations are made at different time periods instead of a single time period as in the case of a cross-sectional study. Longitudinal studies are more concerned with patterns over time.

There are three types of longitudinal studies: trend, cohort and panel studies. Trend studies are concerned with changes within a population over a specified time period. An example would be the changes in voting attitudes according to constituency in Trinidad and Tobago during the course of an election campaign.

Cohort studies are concerned with "more specific sub-populations (cohorts) as they change over time" [Babbie 1992: 99]. Usually when we refer to cohorts we are referring to age groups. Thus a cohort study may include a sample of persons between the ages of 15–20 in 1980, another sample of persons between the ages of 25–30 in 1990, and a third one in 2000, for persons between the ages of 35–40. With this design, the researcher could be following the same group of persons from 1980 to 2000 and be able to compare on any variable of interest. This would then be termed a panel study as this design allows the researcher to examine the same set of persons over time.

Cohort studies are concerned with studying specific groups over time, but not the same persons. Panel studies, on the other hand, are concerned with studying the same group of persons over time. Take another example: a sample of students interviewed every year for the next three or four years of their university life on their attitudes towards tertiary education would constitute a panel study. We could then begin to look at whether the views have changed and perhaps identify what are the critical events which have contributed to these changes. The advantage of the panel study over the others is its ability to show precisely, changes in attitudes over time. This happens because of its ability to study the same set of respondents instead of (as in the case of cohort studies) different samples. While longitudinal studies are usually preferred to cross-sectional studies, they often require an extensive outlay of time and resources.

The experiment

Our discussion on research design would not be complete without referring to the classical explanatory design. As we have pointed out, the beginner-researcher is best advised to steer clear of this design as questions of cause are so difficult to address. We will, however, briefly point to the features that require the researcher to be more experienced and be conversant with more advanced methodologies. The experiment is the most effective design for establishing causal relationships between variables. The concern of the experiment is to introduce control over what may be termed contaminating factors.

A study carried out in Kingston, Jamaica by Eleanor Wint and Janet Brown [1986] utilized an experimental design in an attempt to identify key factors which influence the learning of effective parenting. One requirement of the experimental design was the random allocation of respondents to the control group or the test group. In other words, since all the subjects were similar, by some scientific method of allocation, some subjects were to be exposed to one type of training while others were not. The social reality of the respondents, however, intervened and suddenly the researchers realized that this method of random selection to either the control or the experimental group had caused persons from neighbouring yards to be in different groups. These same persons were therefore able to go home, and at night or over the weekend have a good discussion about all that had transpired in the training sessions.

This then became a contaminating factor which made it difficult for the researchers to make causal statements about the relationship between the variables in this case.

One of the advantages of control over the research environment is that the researcher can use smaller samples in his or her study. However, there are limitations associated with experiments. First, because of control, true experiments operate in an unnatural environment. As a result it is often difficult to simulate the natural environment as there is the tendency for researchers to simplify the context in which human behaviour operates. The fact is that human behaviour is very complex and can be affected by small changes to the environment. Because of our 'social selves' we tend to react to different situations in different ways. We might even react differently to the same situation each time it occurs.

The second limitation associated with the experiment is that which we term the 'reactive' effect where the experimenter's expectations actually lead him or her to produce findings in conformity with such expectations. This reactive effect may be the result of a relationship between the subject and the experimenter where the experimenter unconsciously gives cues to the subject in relation to how he or she should behave.

In the social sciences, experiments are mostly associated with psychological or psycho-social studies. Psychology and social work as disciplines deal with individuals and small groups which are more suitable for the experimental method. Sociology, economics, political and management sciences on the other hand, tend to be more concerned with making conclusions about large groups.

Main Points

📖 Theories are general propositions which attempt to explain a particular situation which can then be empirically observed. A theory is critical in the implementation of scientific research.

📖 Concepts and constructs are the building blocks of a theory. They are generalized ideas about an entire class of objective and subjective phenomena, respectively. Concepts and constructs are an integral part of empirical reasoning. The level of abstraction in the defining of these concepts or constructs will however, influence the research design selected.

📖 The three different types of research design are the exploratory, the descriptive/formative and the explanatory. The main areas of difference between these designs relate to the stringency of sampling, method of data collection and the statistical tests employed in analysis.

📖 In order to choose the best research design we must bear in mind the research intent, the accessibility of the sample and the resources available to the researcher.

Exercise 1

State whether you think the researcher is employing a deductive or inductive type of reasoning in the following examples.

1. Longitudinal observations of teenage mothers' behaviour in an effort to predict the occurrence of teenage pregnancy in adolescent youth.

2. A definition of a 'poverty line' through an examination of a cross-section of the society in terms of the ability to afford basic human needs such as shelter, education, health and food.

3. A comparison of manufacturing firms in the garment industry across the Caricom region with a view to distinguishing effective management styles.

How to zero in on a problem

Research Topic: Select a relevant topic.

Step 1... Identify interest area.

Step 2... Define descriptors within the interest area: These would include the major concepts with which you are concerned, e.g. types of administration, organization of halls, definitions of campus life, student satisfaction.

Step 3... Select key words which help with library searches.

Step 4... Discuss interest with students and administrators.

Step 5... Remember why you are doing the study.

When you have located reference sources in the library, remember to use a proper bibliographic reference so as to make your final listing of references a simple process. Remember the sequence above: read, note, read, discuss, note, read again and then try and take a position. The literature helps to sensitize you to those concepts and constructs already identified by other researchers as being important. It also sensitizes you to the gaps which exist in both theory and application. Reading also provides you with other potential references and methodologies which help you with formulating your own design.

After reading a book, for example, if you find it very useful, prepare your own abstract – usually on a card or small piece of paper. This prevents plagiarism. It also helps to list particular variables of interest. Underline or list these and notice how they are termed and measured. This guards against bigotry and perceptual sets.

Do not trust memory; write down those additional thoughts that come to you which will help you with further searching. The whole purpose is to reduce the topic area identified to a manageable practice level.

Do you recall the format for references? Perhaps revision would be useful.

What if literature is short?

There may be a sparse collection of relevant academic literature, but there may also be a number of popular sources. Both routes will contribute to clarity of perception and help you to conceptualize your research focus. Popular sources often make easy reading. They also often suggest contemporary and sometimes innovative or revolutionary ways of conceptualizing problems and solutions. Popular sources combined with experienced practitioners' views will often open our minds to new perspectives. However, we should regard these views as part of the literature review, quoting from them verbatim in the same way that we would from books and journals. Their views should not be confused in the report with the data gathered, the findings.

Chapter Three

Hypothesis Testing and the Research Proposal

Acceptance of the scientific method usually forces the researcher into an orderly and logical sequencing of actions. As is clear from the Figure of the research process on page 5, to move on to operationalization, the researcher needs to be quite clear about (i) the concepts under consideration, and (ii) the relationship which is of interest. These answers often result in the formulation of a research question. However, in order to make the transition from theory to operationalization, the research question needs to be framed not simply in conceptual terms but more importantly in a functional sense (see Figure 1.1).

The language of conceptualization is a theoretical one, whereas the language of hypothesis testing transforms the theories or assumptions into concrete and empirical terms, to be tested.

The Hypothesis

The term 'thesis' refers to a proposition or statement that can be supported by argument and evidence. The Greek prefix *hypo* means beneath or underlying. Using these meanings, a hypothesis then becomes a non-obvious statement that makes an assertion. The hypothesis is stated in a form that establishes a testable base about a doubtful or unknown statement. Of course, for social science research total proof is impossible, but we can certainly reduce enough of human and mechanical error and doubt to entertain the relationship stated in the hypothesis.

Thus, the hypothesis is a statement that can be tested. It is, more precisely, a statement of a relationship between two or more concepts (or variables). It must be worded in a way that it can be either rejected or not rejected. In other words, you either do not have evidence to support it (reject) or you do (do not reject).

With the research hypothesis, the use of clear wording helps the researcher to minimize personal bias. As we all know, words and concepts have different meanings to each of us. We should therefore be careful to identify for the users of the research (and of course for ourselves), the meaning that is particular to this piece of research. This precise wording serves to avoid ambiguity and interpretation.

The stage of hypothesis formulation is critical to the research process. Any unclear assumptions set the pace for the research, leading to inaccurate, erroneous and unacceptable findings. As we said earlier on, making the transition from conceptualization to operationalization is a logical procedure which follows a specific sequence.

Let us posit four questions which we wish to transform into hypotheses:

1. Do particular areas of St Andrew, Jamaica, i.e. areas with a marked predominance of black people, show a unique type of income distribution?

2. Are low income women motivated to seek skills-training?

3. Does socio-economic status of the partner bear any relationship to the likelihood of domestic violence occurring?

4. Does height affect choice regarding class leadership amongst elementary school children?

Formulation of the hypothesis

If we look at the first question we find that we have two concepts: one is the predominance of black people in a particular population while the other is the level of income. The hypothesis when stated should reflect a relationship between these two concepts so that the behaviour of one will most likely lead to a change in behaviour of the other. Diagrammatically the hypothesis can be represented thus:

[race of person] + [level of income]

The + or – sign represents a positive or a negative relationship between the two concepts; thus if we had a + sign as below

[race of person] + [level of income]

we would say 'having a predominance of black people in the specific population is associated with higher levels of income'. This diagram helps us to see the suggested relationship between the concepts represented in the hypothesis.

We could even go on to qualify the relationship adding some indication of strength or direction. Thus, having a predominance of black people in the specific population is directly proportional to higher levels of income.

In the second question, the two concepts in which we are interested are:

[income of women] and [motivation to seek skills-training].

Now if we make this into a hypothesis, we would first put in an arrow and a sign to indicate the direction of the relationship as well as the type of relationship. Thus:

[income of women] → [motivation to seek skills-training]

Here, if the income of women changes then their motivation to seek skills training should also change but in the opposite direction. The hypothesis would then be stated thus – as the income of women increases their motivation to seek skills-training falls.

Perhaps you could try to represent the relationship between the two concepts as a positive one, using the boxes below.

[   ] → [   ]

Hypothesis formulation is not difficult if we follow the steps. First, two concepts of concern must be clearly stated. The next step is a decision as to which of them you wish to cause, lead to, affect, be associated with, be related to, or influence the other. These are the terms most frequently used to interpret the various types of relationships which we will encounter.

What Are Variables?

From time to time we have used the word variable. When speaking of the hypothesis, we are more accustomed to hearing of a relationship between variables rather than a relationship between concepts. A variable is therefore something which can change and can be measured. For instance, territory of origin and educational qualification are two variables which impact directly on grade point average on graduation from the UWI. We can measure both of these quite easily.

Take the example of educational qualification. We would probably consider whether the person has 'A' levels (number of), tertiary level or additional certification as categories of educational qualification. Another example is the variable of gender. Male and female are the most common indicators of gender grouping and are therefore termed attributes of that variable. Variables are logical groupings of attributes.

Occupation is a variable which can be given different attributes depending on the researcher's interest. Attributes might therefore be farmer, pilot, housewife, stevedore. In another instance the same variable might have the attributes of skilled and unskilled, professional, managerial. A clear ident-ification of the attributes then becomes the logical sequel to the statement of the variable.

It is critical to state both variables and attributes in succinct fashion from the outset so as to be sure what it is about the variable that is changing. For instance, in our earlier example, is it the number of 'A' levels attained, the grade which the student has gained in those subjects, or a combination of both, that is of interest? What is it that is changing? Another way to see variables is as the operational definition of any concept or construct. Remember concepts are the building blocks of theories. In contributing to the formulation of the theory they have already become a part of the definitional statement. The transformation to the variable has simply served to make the concepts more concrete and measurable.

Numerical values

When we speak of variables as measurable, the presence of numbers is suggested. These numbers are the 'real' representations of the value. A value is a specific category or a number descriptive of the degree to which the case studied possesses the variable being assessed. If we are measuring income, then the operationalized variable could be the salary of the respondent, for example, $0–$500, $501–$1,000, $1,001–$1,500. We would then realize a range of income values from EC$0 to EC$1,500. Dollars would be the value used. Numerical values are of two kinds, namely discrete and continuous. Discrete values take only the value of a whole number. For example – Question: How many children do you have? Response: One and one on the way. The correct answer would be one child.

Continuous variables take on any value for which a numerical scheme exists – for example, decimals or fractions. An example of a question might be: How long have you been living here? And the response: Five–and–a–half years.

Values can be related to each other in a dependent fashion or they can stand independently of each other. In this way we will find that the value given to a variable will influence the level of measurement.

It is important to bear in mind that concepts can be transformed into variables in many ways. The measure chosen will depend on: (a) what measures are available at the time (this relates to the level of observation which will be discussed later); (b) what measures have been used in past research; and (c) what measures have been shown to be adequate.

Variable names

Naming variables in research is not as simple as it seems, as the name given has to be concise, sticking precisely to the research focus/intent. The naming of the variable is at the same time necessary for and a result of efficient operationalization.

In the research process we should attempt to name the variable early in the hypothesis testing stage.

Operationalization

Translation of the variable into measurable terms is not a simple task. It challenges the researcher to ensure that what is being measured is in fact the same as the concept. In fact, we more often achieve a measure that explains or represents some part of the concept. The operationalized concept, therefore, remains specific for that particular piece of research, capturing those features which are most important.

An example of this attempt to bridge the gap between the language of conceptualization and the practice of science is the popular concept of social class. Derek Gordon's work [1989] operationalized social class as a composite of indicators. In other words, he first saw social class as being equivalent to socio-economic status, then he brought together a number of indicators, namely social mobility, father's occupation, level of education and geographic residence, to form a measurable indication of socio-economic status.

When we examine this procedure what seems to be of concern is the need to decide what should be measured as well as how it will be measured. If we are going to examine father's occupation, then it means that we must decide how to categorize the occupational groupings. Skilled versus unskilled gives significantly different detail from farmer, horse trainer or higgler/huckster.

An operational definition, therefore, sets out the rules for measurement of that variable. It is a definition which states clearly the procedures which will be used for the measurement of the variables. Operationalization allows us to transform abstract concepts into concrete phenomena which can be measured.

An operational definition tells us how the variable behaves, what it looks like and how it operates. In order to achieve this there are certain guidelines which can be followed.

Do not use synonyms. For example, 'upset' operationalized as feeling sad. Here, we still do not know how you observe being sad. Is it having a made-up face or is it crying steadily through the day? Not only do we need to know what being upset looks like, but we also need to know how to observe and measure it.

Do not use dictionary definitions. An operational definition "is a definition based on the observable characteristics of that which is being defined" [Tuckman 1978: 79]. Some examples from student studies might help to make this more clear:

Conflict – state produced by placing two or more persons in a situation where each has the same goal, but only one can attain it. The operational definition would include a measurable score on a specific scale.

Inmates – persons who are presently residents of local state prisons.

Death row – special section of St Catherine District Prison where men convicted for murder await execution by hanging.

Anxiety – an emotional state with associated feelings of dread, fear and uncertainty, measurable by a score on the Taylor Manifest Anxiety Scale.

Speeding – evidenced by exceeding 50 kph in a marked zone.

Speeding – exceeding 50 kph in a marked zone when children are in or near the street.

Thus it is clear that an operational definition needs to be as simple as possible. The more complex the definition is for observation, the more likely it is that the researcher may commit errors. Simplicity also helps those using the research. Although the definition might be specific to the study, as it must be, the findings of the study may well serve to throw light on a peculiar behaviour which is of interest to other researchers in similar settings. If we are unable to understand the definition and the method of measurement then the usefulness of the study becomes limited. In fact, this type of criticism of the research may well lead to cries of 'invalid', 'unreliable' and perhaps the non-acceptance of the results.

The research proposal

So far we have been looking at the different stages of the research process. An important stage in that process is the development of a research proposal. The research proposal is a document detailing the research intent, the methodology to be employed which will generate the supportive data, and the total costing of the project.

Without proposals, the task of researcher could become confused and non-directive – a feature that would certainly add to the cost and quality of the project.

The research proposal format usually includes the full headings:

- The problem statement and its parameters
- Significance of the research
- Review of the literature or background
- Hypothesis formulation (problem definition)
- Research design and methodology
- Analysis
- Personnel management
- Cost and business arrangements

The research proposal is not cast in stone; it is not inflexible. We should be open to adjustments to the research process even though the intent is to maintain the conceptual design. The proposal, however, does help to keep the process on track within specified time lines and cost limits.

In writing a proposal, show respect for the reader. Keep it short, focused and written in your best language:

- avoid the passive tense
- use active verbs
- avoid run-on sentences
- avoid jargon and mnemonics
- do not use three long words when one short one would do
- avoid abstract and sterile generalizations (verisimilitude)

You will find that when preparing the proposal you might well rewrite the research question after completing the literature review. As the information in the proposal is interrelated this is acceptable. If you recall, formulation of the problem is a challenging task and occasions the use of a great deal of paper. The critical point is the creation of the proposal as the guide to the process. In many cases it is this document which becomes the measure against which the outcome is judged.

Questions that will assist in the preparation of the proposal headings include:

Problem statement and its parameters

What do you intend to study?
Why is it worth studying?
What are the boundaries to this statement?
Can you frame a question which covers the most important aspects of the research topic?

Significance of the research

Could the findings be implemented in a project or programme?
Does the study bring new light to an often discussed relationship?
Is there a significant theoretical refinement brought out in the study, or does it bring new theoretical depth to practice?

At this level however (introductory social research) it is more likely that the greatest significance will be fulfilment of a course requirement within a programme at a tertiary institution.

Review of the literature or background

One outcome of this section is the creation of a list of references or a bibliography which will be appended to the proposal and will reflect the full range of sources used.

How are the concepts represented in the readings?
What are the other pieces of research related to this topic which you have encountered?
Are there major theories encountered and what do they say?
Do the findings and the theories of these studies converge or diverge?
How well do these findings and theories fit your present research intent?
Do you find any inconsistencies or apparently illogical conclusions with which you might take issue?
Can you establish the context or the background to your study?

Hypothesis formulation (problem definition)

Your hypothesis should now flow logically from a discussion of the literature. Remember, not all studies use hypotheses.

Be sure to allow your hypothesis to flow smoothly and logically from gaps in theory and research you have reviewed. Alternatively, you may want to construct a hypothesis which seeks to replicate a study.

Methodology

As far as methodology is concerned, the following issues should be considered.
Sample.
Who and/or what are being studied?
The sources for the primary and secondary data.
What type of sampling method will be used?

Measurement

What are the key variables?
Define and say how variables will be measured.
How do your definitions and measurement methods differ from previous research?

Data collection methods

Who will collect the data?
How will the data be collected and over what time period?
Will the data be collected by a survey or field research?
What type of measurement instrument will be used?

Analysis

What type of analytical approach will be used? Will the analysis be mainly descriptive or causal?
What types of statistical analyses will be used?
What is the logic behind the analysis?
How will the analysis help in answering the research question?

Schedule or time frame

How long will the research take?
Give an outline of time for each stage of the research.

Budget

How much will the study cost?
Give a breakdown of the various expenditures involved in doing the study – for instance, the cost of printing questionnaires, conducting the fieldwork, and printing of reports.

Main Points

- A hypothesis is a statement that explains a phenomenon. It states a relationship between two or more variables which can be tested.

- Hypotheses are worded in a way that they can be either accepted or rejected.

- Hypotheses are used in explanatory studies.

- A variable is a concept that changes and can be measured.

- In order to test a hypothesis the variables need to be operationalized. Operationalization refers to a process which outlines how the variables in a study will be measured.

- An important stage in the research process is the development of a research proposal. The research proposal is a document detailing the research intent, the methodology to be employed which will generate the supportive data and the total costing of the project.

- Without a proposal, the task of the research is made much more difficult.

1. How do you differentiate between the language of hypothesis testing and the language of operationalization? At what stages of the research process are these employed?

2. Develop a hypothesis to test the relationship between the following variables:
   - socio-economic status and attitude towards the party in power
   - ethnic origin and food preferences
   - birth order, domestic abuse and family structure
   - number of children fathered and attitude towards parenting

Chapter Four

Measurement and Sampling

Measurement is the process which allows researchers to take abstract concepts and test them empirically. It should be noted that when we measure variables (e.g. social class) our indicators (e.g. income, education) are only approximations of the variables. In order to measure a concept we have to quantify it. The most effective way to do this is by assigning numbers to the variable. Some variables are easier to measure than others. For instance, 'income' is usually much easier to measure than 'political ideology'. Yet all numbers assigned to the variables should not be interpreted in the same way. We know that a person who earns an income of $100 a week has a smaller income than someone who earns $5,000 per week. However, we cannot say with certainty that someone who goes to church five times per week is less religious than someone who goes to church seven times per week. To cite another example, we can say that a per capita income of $12,000 is six times higher than a per capita income of $2,000. Yet we cannot say that someone who is a Catholic is two times more religious than someone who is a Protestant. To help us sort out some of the problems in measuring variables, researchers classify data into various levels of measurement: nominal, ordinal, interval and ratio.

Nominal variables

Variables classified as nominal have the attributes of exhaustiveness and mutual exclusiveness. Nominal variables are also called categorical variables because they are based on a classification system. To measure nominal variables there must be at least two cases. For instance, the variable 'sex' has the two mutually exclusive and exhaustive cases of 'male' and 'female'. Likewise the variable 'religion' can have mutually exclusive and exhaustive cases of 'Baptist', 'Rastafarian', 'Catholic' and 'Hindu'. In both of these examples a person cannot fit into more than one category. Nominal variables are usually associated with qualitative studies. However, by assigning numbers to represent characteristics of nominal variables, qualitative data can be converted to quantitative data.

Ordinal variables

Ordinal variables are similar to nominal variables in that they have mutually exclusive and exhaustive categories. However, they are different because these categories are rank ordered and follow a logical order. For example, 'social class' may be considered an ordinal variable if we measure it according to 'upper', 'middle' and 'lower' categories. In this classification we rank 'middle' above 'lower' and 'upper' above 'middle' in terms of social status and economic well-being. We are not necessarily making value judgments about the desirability of a particular category, but instead their relative positions on the socio-economic ladder in society. Another example of an ordinal variable is 'size of city' which can be ranked as 'small', 'medium' and 'large'.

Interval and ratio variables

Interval and ratio levels measurement are not only rank ordered but they also indicate exact distances between the categories. Examples of interval level measurements include weight measured in grams and examination scores measured in percentages. With interval and ratio levels of measures the distance between 10 and 20 metres is the same as that between 40 and 50. Furthermore, with interval and ratio measurements the numbers have real meaning. Thus, someone who scores 30 percent in an exam has only half as many marks as someone with 60 percent.

There is one difference between interval and ratio levels of measurement. Variables measured on a ratio scale have a true zero while those measured intervally do not. One example of a measure without a true zero is intelligence quotient (IQ) measured by scores received on an IQ test. If someone scores 0 on an IQ test, it does not mean that that person has no IQ. An example of a ratio scale is dollars and cents. It is possible for someone to have zero dollars or zero cents.

Reliability and Validity

As we have stated above, the job of the social researcher is to try to capture reality as truthfully as possible in his or her research. Indicators help us to concretize complex concepts. We should note that these indicators are only approximations of reality. A social researcher can never truly measure 'social class' since there are qualitative dimensions to this concept which elude quantification. Notwithstanding this limitation social researchers attempt to maximize precision and accuracy in conducting research. A measurement may be precise but not necessarily accurate. For example, to say that popular Jamaican entertainer Buju Banton is West Indian and Trinidadian is more precise than saying that he is simply West Indian. However, because Buju is Jamaican and not Trinidadian, the statement that he is West Indian is more accurate. When researchers refer to precision and accuracy they are talking about reliability and validity.

Reliability

Reliability refers to whether a particular technique yields the same results repeatedly when applied to a research question. For instance, if a pollster conducted a poll in a particular area on three different occasions and got the same results each time, we would conclude that the technique he or she used was reliable. Take another example, suppose you weighed yourself five different times on a bathroom scale and got the same results each time we would conclude that the scale is reliable. Even if the scale were adjusted to give the same incorrect weight each time, it would still be reliable.

There are three common ways to test for reliability. The first is known as the *test-retest method*. This method involves taking a measurement more than once and then comparing the results. If the results from the different tests vary then it indicates that the measurement is unreliable. For example, to test whether or not an examination is a reliable measure of academic performance, a test may be administered on two separate occasions to members of the same group. The scores for each test are then compared to see if they are consistent. If they are not significantly different we would conclude the examination is reliable. A popular alternative to the test-retest method is known as the *alternative test*. Here, instead of giving the same test twice, a comparable test is administered and the results are also compared.

The second is the *split-half method* which involves dividing indicators of an instrument into two equal groups, and then comparing the correlations for each group. If the correlations for each group are different then we would conclude that the instrument is not very reliable. For example, suppose you developed a set of twelve items to measure the concept of political ideology. To apply the split-half method you would randomly assign each item to two groups of six and compare the results from each group. Each group should measure the concept in basically the same way. If the results of the two groups vary significantly then there is a problem of reliability.

The third technique is simply using *established measures* which have been already tested and proven. For instance, two established measures of the concept 'social class' are 'income' and 'occupation of respondent'. One useful way of arriving at an established measure is through the literature review, especially of research reports and scientific articles.

Validity

Validity refers to the extent to which an empirical measure actually measures the concept which it purports to measure. While reliability is related to precision, validity refers to accuracy. If we use the example of the bathroom scale, for the measurement to be valid it has to accurately reflect the true weight of the person being weighed. There are three main types of validity. There is criterion-related validity which refers to the extent to which the results of a test have predictive power. For instance, a driver's test is supposed to be a good predictor of driving ability. Second, there is content validity which refers to the extent to which a measure or set of measures covers the entire range of the subject matter under study. For instance, a sociology examination has a high level of content validity if it covers all of the subject areas of the course. Third, there is construct validity which refers to the relationship between variables from a theoretical standpoint. For instance, let us say that you are doing a study on deviance. You develop a measure of deviance (high and low deviance), and you have various expectations about deviance – for example, people who do not receive parental socialization are more likely to have a high level of deviance. If from your empirical research your measure of deviance relates in the expected way, then we would conclude that the study has high construct validity.

Internal and external validity

There are some studies which may be high on internal validity but low on external validity. Researchers prefer high internal and external validity. Internal validity refers to "whether or not an apparent difference can be explained away as some measurement, artifact . . . external validity is the problem of interpreting the difference, the problem of generalization" [Webb 1966 quoted in Bailey 1987: 70]. Internal validity therefore focuses on contradictions in the data of a particular study, while external validity is concerned with the extent to which the findings can be generalized beyond the subjects of the particular research [Bailey 1987].

Scales and Indices

Sociologists and psychologists have developed a number of instruments for measuring attitudes, perceptions, feelings and so on. In recent years there has been an explosion of the literature in this area. In this book we deal with this issue cursorily, since there are numerous sources which deal with this topic more comprehensively. According to Babbie [1989: 390] the terms index and scales are often "used imprecisely and interchangeably in social research literature". He further states that indices are constructed through the simple accumulation of scores assigned to individual attributes. For instance, the Human Development Index (HDI) is a composite of three components of human development: longevity, knowledge and standard of living. The three components of the HDI are combined into an overall index score which is expressed as a value between 0 and 1.

A scale is constructed through the assignment of scores to patterns of attributes. Social researchers usually prefer scales over indices because they convey more information than index scores. Before a social researcher uses either a scale or an index it should be validated and tested for reliability. Over the years a number of statistical techniques have been developed for these purposes. Three of the most commonly used scaling methods are Social Distance, Likert and Semantic Differential.

Good scales should have the following characteristics [Oppenheim 1992]:

1. Uni-dimensionality – the scale should measure one thing at a time. That is to say the items in the scale should be internally cohesive.

2. Reliability – the scale should produce consistent results each time as long as the context remains the same.

3. Validity – the scale should measure what it purports to measure.

4. Linearity – there should be equal intervals between categories thus making quantitative scoring possible.

Social distance scale

The social distance scale, often called the Borgardus Social Distance scale (named after its inventor in 1925) is one of the most widely used scales in social research. The scale is aimed at measuring the degree and intensity of social distance between different groups of people. Suppose a researcher wanted to study the extent to which people of, say, Guyana are willing to associate with people of Antigua, he or she might decide to use a scale like the crudely constructed one below.

- I would exclude all Antiguans from my country   1
- I am willing to permit Antiguans to visit my country   2
- I am willing to permit Antiguans to live in my country   3
- I am willing to permit Antiguans to live in my community   4
- I am willing to permit Antiguans to live next door to me   5
- I am willing to permit Antiguans to marry members of my family   6

Notice that as we move from item 1 to item 6, the intensity of acceptance is greater. Hence, if most of the Guyanese respondents circle all of the items, it reflects a relatively favourable level of acceptance of Antiguans.

Likert scale

Another way of measuring attitudes is with the Likert scale. The Likert scale is a system of measurement associated with a questionnaire format, which requires the respondent to answer along a continuum – 'strongly disagree', 'disagree', 'neutral', 'agree', 'strongly agree'. Let us say that a researcher wishes to measure racial attitudes in the Caribbean, he or she might use the following items as part of the scale:

	SA	A	N	D	SD
1. The Caribbean is a melting pot of races:	1	2	3	4	5
2. In the Caribbean a person's racial origin does not determine his/her life chances:	1	2	3	4	5

Respondents are supposed to indicate one of the responses – SA (strongly agree), A (agree), N (neutral), D (disagree) and SA (strongly disagree) – each of which is assigned a score. The scores are then tallied and used to perform an item analysis to select those items which are best suited to measure the variable. A scale is then constructed from the average index score of each item.

While very few social researchers use the Likert scales, many find the Likert questionnaire format quite appealing. Usually, the researcher simply constructs an index by summing the scores from each item into an overall total. This index score is used to represent a relative measure of the attitude being studied.

Semantic Differential

An alternative to the Likert scale is known as the Semantic Differential scale. This scale requires respondents to decide between two extreme positions or opposites. Assume that you are a management consultant who decides to educate consumers about a new product on the market by giving talks to audiences around the country. One way to gauge the effectiveness of these talks is by using the Semantic Differential scale, similar to the one below.

How would you rate the talk ?
Boring — — — — — Stimulating
Informative — — — — — Uninformative
Unenlightening — — — — — Enlightening

One of the advantages of the Semantic Differential scale is that it gives the researcher a fairly clear idea about the intensity of feelings. In the case of the marketing expert or researcher it is important to capture clearly which end of the scale consumers are more likely to be.

[For a more detailed discussion of this issue see Earl Babbie, *The Practice of Social Research*, (California: Wadsworth Publishing Co. 1989 ; Kenneth Bailey,) *Methods of Social Research* (New York: The Free Press, 1987); and A. N. Oppenheim, *Questionnaire Design, Interviewing and Attitude Measurement* (London: Printer Publishers, 1992)].

Sampling

In 1989, Professor Carl Stone accurately predicted the outcome of the Jamaica general elections. To make this prediction Stone interviewed a small fraction of the eligible voters in the country. You may ask, how is it possible for someone to use a small fraction of a population to make statements about the entire population? To answer this question we need to understand the process of sampling. Sampling may be described as the process of selecting observations from a population. Statisticians have been able to develop ways to draw conclusions about populations from samples. Such samples allow us to also calculate our margin of error, as is done in political polling.

There are basically two types of sampling: probability and non-probability.

Probability sampling

Probability samples are those in which we know the probability (or chance factor) for the selection of the sampling units. This is obtained by some kind of randomization procedure. These samples assume that the mean of the sample is equal to the mean of the population under study. Its advantages include avoidance of the conscious or unconscious biases of the researcher in selecting the sampling units and allowance for precise measurements of sampling errors.

Probability sampling is divided into four basic types:

1. Simple random sampling

2. Stratified random sampling

3. Systematic random sampling

4. Multi-stage (cluster or area) sampling

All the types assume some degree of prior knowledge about the population being studied. A sampling frame puts parameters around, and defines the population from which the sample is selected. It is normally a listing of all individuals/items in the population under study.

Simple Random Sampling

In simple random sampling each person or item has an equal chance of being chosen. Here the chance of selection must be known in advance and a random method of selection is used to determine the items selected such as a table of random numbers (see Appendix 3) or the lottery method. To use the table of random numbers method, the members of the population are numbered from one to N and N members are drawn from the table of random numbers. The numbers drawn from the table then become the sample. With the lottery method, a name or number of each member of the population is placed in a bag or suitable container and well mixed, and a sample of the required size is then draw.

It should be noted that the term simple random sampling refers to sampling 'without replacement'. That is, each item selected from the population is not replaced in the population before another draw is made. This prevents the same item from appearing in the sample more than once. On the other hand, random sampling 'with replacement' is known as 'unrestricted random sampling'. Although most statistical theory relates to unrestricted random sampling, in general, social researchers use simple random sampling (or sampling without replacement) because it produces more precise estimators [Moser and Kalton 1986: 81 – 82]. An estimator is a numerical approximation of a population parameter. For example, the mean income computed from a sample of workers in a factory may be used as estimator for the actual mean income of the population of workers in the factory.

Stratified Random Sampling

Often a population contains various distinct groups or strata which differ on the attribute that is being researched. Stratified random sampling involves sampling each stratum separately to increase precision, or reduce time, effort and cost by allowing smaller sample sizes for a given level of precision. With respect to the variable under study it is best to stratify each stratum that is internally homogeneous (intra-strata homogeneity) but heterogeneous with respect to each other (inter-strata heterogeneity). When the sampling fractions of each stratum are equal, it is a *proportional stratified sample*. For example, if we know that there are 600 Baptists, 300 Catholics and 100 Rastafarians in a given population, a proportional stratified sample would consist of 60 Baptists, 30 Catholics, and 10 Rastafarians. Here the sampling fraction is equal (1/10) for all three strata which also exist proportionate to the sampling frame.

If the sampling fractions are unequal, it is a *disproportional stratified sample*. For example, if we wanted to compare the three major religious groups with respect to their attendance at religious functions, we could manipulate the sampling fraction to make the design more effective. If we took 50 from each religious group, the sampling fractions would be 1/12, 1/6, 1/2. In a disproportional stratified sample, the disproportional stratified samples are useful for comparisons, and allow for different distribution of economic costs for different strata.

Systematic Random Sampling

Systematic random sampling is similar to random sampling but instead of using a table of random numbers to select individual items, this method uses a predetermined systematic procedure. Here a list of the sampling frame is necessary. To draw a systematic sample the researcher takes a list, calculates a sampling fraction, determines a random start and then selects every k^{th} item until he or she has arrived at his or her sample. Thus if there were 1,000 persons in a population and the required sample size was 100, the sample fraction would be 1,000/100 which is every 10th item. The researcher would arrive at a random start between 1 and 10 and then sample every 10th element on the list until he or she reaches 100. Systematic samples are usually better to use in the field and hence subject to fewer errors than either simple or stratified samples. They also provide better information per unit cost than the simple random sample. Whenever there is an ordering of a list that is random with regard to the variables being measured, a systematic random sample is equal to a simple random sample.

However, with this type of sampling, there are possible sources of bias. First, if the individuals or items are ordered so that a trend occurs, this may affect the results. Secondly, if the list has some periodic/cyclical characteristics that correspond to the sampling fraction, it may result in a systematic bias in selection or non-selection of items.

Multi-stage (Cluster or Area) Sampling

Multi-stage sampling involves an initial sampling of clusters, followed by the sub-sampling of members of each cluster or group. Cluster sampling is normally used when it is impossible, difficult or expensive to obtain an exhaustive list of elements of a population. For example, suppose we wanted to do a study of Muslims in Trinidad and Tobago. We might decide that our target population are those persons who attend mosques regularly. Now although there is no exhaustive list of persons who attend mosques in Trinidad and Tobago, Muslims in that country attend distinct mosques. Using a cluster approach we would then construct a list of mosques, and then sample them using one of the many probability sampling techniques. That is the first stage of sampling. In the second stage we would obtain a list of the members of each mosque selected, and then draw a random sample of each of them. This type of sample is known as a two-stage cluster sample. There are more complex types of samples which involve many more stages of sampling. Multi-stage cluster sampling therefore involves listing and sampling at each stage.

One of the problems with cluster sampling is that it tends to introduce more error than other types of probability samples. Every item we sample introduces error in the analysis. Because multi-stage cluster sampling involves sampling more than once, this tends to compound the number of errors, consequently reducing the accuracy of the sample.

Non-probability sampling

Non-probability samples are characterized by the unavailability of ways to estimate the chance factor of each sample unit to be included in the sample. They do not use techniques for randomization, nor do they assume the mean of the sampling distribution is equal to the mean of the sample. They are used when a list of the population (sampling frame) does not exist. They are convenient and inexpensive, but are limited by serious threats to external validity. Their limitations, however, can be lessened by exercising caution and expertise and by replication of the studies. Non-probability sampling includes the following:

1. Accidental Sampling
2. Judgemental (Purposive) Sampling
3. Quota Sampling
4. Snowball (Mudball) Sampling
5. Dense Sampling
6. Saturation Sampling

Accidental Sampling

Accidental sampling, as the name connotes, is a sample drawn accidentally, purely for reasons of convenience and accessibility. They are not generalizable and are useful for pilot testing.

Judgemental (Purposive) Sampling

In judgemental sampling the researcher uses experts to choose samples that are representative based upon their expertise and prior knowledge. In other words, the distinguishing feature of this sampling is that the researcher uses his or her own judgement (or the judgement of experts) as to whom to select and how many, based on the aims of the research project and prior knowledge of the population and its elements.

Quota Sampling

Quota sampling is in many ways equivalent to stratified sampling. This technique involves stratifying the population and sampling each stratum proportionate to its representation in the population. For instance, suppose we wanted to do a study of race/ethnic relations in Barbados, and the census reports showed that 80 percent of the population was black, 16 percent was mixed, 3 percent was white and 1 percent was of East Indian origin. Let us say that we require a sample which reflects the proportions of each racial/ethnic group in the population. Therefore, if our sample were 1,000, 800 would be black, 160 would be mixed, 30 would be white, and 10 would be of East Indian descent. One caveat, however, is that for purposes of statistical computation, strata that are very small may have to use disproportionate samples.

Quota sampling requires the researcher to be familiar with his or her population. Like other non-probability samples, quota samples suffer from interviewer bias since they allow interviewers a great deal of discretion in choosing their respondents.

Snowball Sampling (Mudball Sampling)

Snowball or 'mudball' sampling is a technique used by researchers to identify and sample an elusive population. However, members of the target population should be in contact with each other formally and informally. The first stage includes interviewing a small number of persons with the required information in the target population and using them as informants to identify other potential respondents in that population. Remember the analogy to a snowball/mudball which begins small but becomes larger as it rolls downhill. The snowball/mudball technique is useful for constructing our literature review.

Dense Sampling

Dense sampling normally includes sampling more than half and less than all the members of a population. This requires a large amount of time and money.

Saturation Sampling

Saturation sampling involves sampling all the elements of a given population and its inclusion within sampling is debated because it does not involve a subset of the population, but the entire population itself.

Public opinion polling

Public opinion polls have now become an integral part of our everyday political discourse. Carl Stone legitimized public opinion polling in Jamaica and had some initial difficulty in trying to convince the public of their validity and usefulness. Fortunately, times have changed and we now use polls to give us some idea of how the public feels about a wide range of issues.

This trend towards capturing the views of members of the public is a good initiative, but it is also important that we become fully aware of the limitations associated with this opinion measuring tool.

One problem associated with political polls is methodology. A poll is a survey conducted on a representative subset or part of a population. Therefore, this subset is supposed to reflect the thinking of the population. The members of this subset are often selected by complex sampling methods which will allow the pollsters to construct an appropriate margin of error which is arrived at with the aid of standard statistical formulas. Thus in order not to affect the validity of polls, the pollsters must ensure that they are representative of the population with an adequate sample size. However, there are other more serious problems associated with surveys which can make the estimation of a margin of error problematic, if based on simply the size of the sample. For example, a simple problem such as the interviewees misunderstanding a question may lead to the introduction of numerous additional errors, thus reducing the validity of the findings.

If a poll is to be regarded as national it should capture and represent the opinions of a wide cross-section of the population. Hence, pollsters should always provide their readers with a description of their sampling procedure. The pollsters should also ensure that the number of persons interviewed is large enough to allow the sample/subset to look/resemble the population/whole. The sample size should really be determined by a case-by-case approach. It is also suggested that pollsters who do not have an intimate understanding of the dynamics of the local political landscape need to examine the sample size and general sampling methodology of competent researchers who are familiar with the situation. Note well, from a statistical point of view a national sample of 500 can have a margin of error plus or minus 4 percent. However, in reality the vagaries of research may introduce many more errors into the findings, consequently widening the 'true' margin of error. Therefore, it is not always wise to base a margin of error simply on standard calculations in a statistical textbook. In general, the greater the number of variables and the more complicated the analysis, the larger the sample should be. Concomitantly, the more complicated the sampling technique and level of analysis, the more difficult it is to estimate a margin of error. Even if we are to accept that the sampling procedure is good, the manner in which questions are asked could lead to results which are not valid – even the best pollster can fall into the trap of asking questions that sometimes lead to biased results. Studies of polls undertaken by leading American polling organizations show that small changes to the wording of questions often lead to very different or conflicting results. As an example we will examine the same question asked in two different ways:

1. Should divorce in this country be easier or more difficult to obtain than now?

2. Should divorce in this country be easier to obtain, more difficult to obtain, or stay as it is now?

According to Floyd Fowler [1988], these two versions of the same question were used in separate surveys among the same population, using similar sample size, but they produced two different sets of results. The reason for the different results is because in the second question, respondents were allowed three optional responses as opposed to two as in the first question. Hence, the availability of additional response categories allows for a greater range of responses, and possibly results.

Another hotly debated aspect of polls is their ability to predict. There is no doubt that polls – given similar circumstances – conducted repeatedly can enable the researcher to predict an outcome. This does not mean that the prediction will always be correct. But if we isolate and establish some patterns in political attitudes over a given period of time, we will be able to use these patterns to predict an outcome – given our understanding of the political landscape. Further, if we are to assume that there is some degree of regularity to human behaviour then there is no reason why we cannot predict that behaviour with some degree of accuracy.

Admittedly, some predictions can be a very hazardous exercise, especially if the results of the polls prove to be inaccurate. Even if the results of the polls are accurate there are other problems which might be the source of serious concern. Polls tend to capture how people feel at a given point in time and, by extension, there is no way of knowing how they will feel at a later date – unless another poll is conducted. Given the dynamics of human attitude and behaviour, it is reasonable to believe that people will change their points of view several times about a single issue. They may change their opinions because of the availability of new information. The more complex the issue the more undecided humans tend to be. However, as the situation begins to unravel then we might begin to take a clearer position. Perhaps the most controversial aspect of public opinion polling is drawing inferences from the results. The reason is that many analysts have argued that it is not clear whether polls reflect what people actually feel or whether they reflect the influence of powerful interest groups on the population. In most modern societies, the most important sources of influences for the adult population are their peers and the media. In many Caricom countries, radio talk shows often set the agenda for discussion while articulating the point of view of the hosts of these programmes.

In societies where information on a number of public issues is often restricted to those who have connections with the powerful, what sometimes passes for objective analysis is often no more than a thinly veiled attempt by those who have access to this information to achieve some personal end. Therefore, what the public may perceive as facts may in fact be incorrect. Social scientists know from research that public opinion can be affected by having a respected and authoritative figure repeat information to the public. Clear examples of this were seen during the 1994 health care bill debate in the United States where those persons who opposed health care reform articulated their position in the media via sundry influential persons. Additionally, the use of scare tactics through the appeal to core American values, such as freedom and responsibility, helped to hammer the point home. This is not to say that all public opinion is formed through the manipulation of information by interest groups since public opinion can also be formed as a result of people's own daily experiences. Furthermore, many of us can disentangle the personal agenda of a talk show host or journalist from the larger issue which affects the country.

Nonetheless, the following questions will assist you in evaluating a poll:

- Who was interviewed?
- How large was the sample?
- What were the questions asked and in what order?
- How were the interviews conducted?
- When were the interviews conducted?
- Who sponsored the poll – and why?

Public opinion polls are fraught with many dangers and shortcomings. However, this does not mean that they are not useful, for they give us an understanding of how the general population feels about an issue at a particular point in time; and how people feel at a given time may be the result of a variety of factors not the least of which being how the poll was conducted. If we understand these influences and seek to examine this opinion measuring tool within this context then we can continue to glean useful insights into public opinion and perhaps even advance the democratic process.

📖 Measurement allows researchers to take abstract concepts and test them empirically. Measurement refers to assigning numbers to variables.

📖 Social researchers classify data into four levels of measurement: nominal, ordinal, interval and ratio.

📖 Nominal variables have the attributes of exhaustiveness and mutual exclusiveness. An example would be religion.

📖 Ordinal variables have attributes of exhaustiveness, mutual exclusiveness with categories that are rank ordered. An example would be social class.

📖 Interval and ratio variables have similar attributes to ordinal variables, but in addition there are exact distances between categories. However, unlike interval variables, variables measured on a ratio scale have true zeros. An example of an interval variable would be IQ, while an example of a ratio variable would be monthly income.

📖 The objective of the social researcher is to capture reality as precisely and accurately as possible.

📖 Social researchers use the terms of reliability and validity to refer to precision and accuracy, respectively.

📖 Reliability is concerned with whether a particular technique yields the same results repeatedly when applied to a research question.

📖 Validity is concerned with the extent to which an empirical measure actually measures the concept it purports to measure.

📖 Sociologists use scales and indices to measure attitudes, perceptions and feelings.

📖 Indices are constructed through the simple accumulation of scores assigned to individual attributes. Scales are constructed through the assignment of scores to patterns of attributes.

📖 Sampling may be described as the process of selecting observations from a population. A sample is a subset of a population.

📖 Probability samples employ random selection mechanisms, which allow the researcher to estimate the sampling error. Examples of probability samples include: simple random, stratified, systematic and multi-stage cluster.

📖 Non-probability samples do not employ random-selection mechanisms, hence the researcher is unable to estimate the sampling error. Examples of non-probability samples include judgement, quota, accidental, snowball/mudball and dense.

📖 Public opinion polls are now used throughout the Caribbean. They provide us an idea of how the public feels about a range of issues.

📖 When assessing a poll care should be taken to find out the following: Who was interviewed? How large was the sample? What questions were asked and how? When were the interviews conducted? Who sponsored the poll and why?

I. The purpose of this exercise is to demonstrate that a random sample is not a haphazard sample; instead there are procedures that must be followed if the sample is to be a probability sample. This exercise has the purpose of giving students some experience in using tables of random numbers to draw such samples.

First Sample: Draw a 5-percent sample of pages from some book that contains at least 300 pages. All of the pages of the book constitute your population; the list of page numbers constitutes your sampling frame; and the page numbers you draw represent your sample. First record those cases that are in your sample then answer the following:

a. How many cases will be in your 5-percent sample? N=

b. How did you select the page and location of the starting point for moving through the table of random numbers? (Note that this is defined before, not after the sample is drawn.)

c. What course of movements (direction) have you chosen to progress through the table of random numbers? (Note that this must also be decided ahead of time to avoid biases for certain types of numbers.)

d. Record those cases that are in your sample.

e. What percent of the pages are even numbers and what percent are odd numbered pages?

f. Did every case in your population have an equal chance of being included in your sample? Why do you say this?

II. What is the most appropriate level of measurement for each of the following variables:

Variable Indicator

a. Religion: Hindu, Catholic, Muslim, Rastafarian

b. Attitudes towards capital punishment: strongly approve, approve, disapprove, strongly disapprove

c. Political ideology: radical, liberal, conservative

d. Age: number of years at last birthday

e. Income: net monthly salary

III. Construct valid and reliable measures for the following concepts. Then construct invalid and unreliable measures for the same concepts. Justify your choices.

a. Emotional state

b. Academic performance

c. Level of patriotism

d. Level of political consciousness

e. Family size

f. Social class

Chapter Five

Qualitative Research

Qualitative research can be described as an approach or an attitude to data gathering, which comprises indepth investigation of human perceptions, attitudes and experiences, as well as the associated processes by, and/or the contexts within which these occur. The approach results in value-added understanding of motivations and behaviours.

This type of research relies on observations and analyses which subjectively measure individuals' introspection, interpersonal interactions, and those with relevant communities, the identification of which is purposive. Processes of reporting for qualitative research are heavily supported by verbal and visual descriptions, quotations, and interpretive coding.

The term 'qualitative research' itself is arguably not a well-known one. Although a few might doubt the accuracy of this statement, it would probably be because they had been fortunate enough to experience the processes and realize the value attached to such investigation methods.

At this stage in the development of the techniques, there is still considerable ignorance regarding definitions, descriptions, and the scope for utilization of qualitative research. In addition, there is relatively little methodological research being conducted on the processes that comprise and validate the methods. There is also comparatively little formal instruction and training being offered in academic settings that relate to the respective qualitative methods.

Much scepticism still abounds with regard to the utility and scientific validity of qualitative research methods. Therefore, one of the first issues usually discussed with respect to qualitative research is its comparative value relative to those of quantitative techniques such as survey methodology. Many proponents of the scientific approach to problem solving would deny that qualitative research has any 'real value'.

Qualitative research actually comprises several methodologies, carrying different nomenclatures including ethnography, observation and interviewing. In more recent times, focus group discussions have been added to the list of practised techniques. Qualitative research is not a new approach to investigation, having been used for cultural research in earlier days by sociologists and anthropologists.

A rebirth of these concepts has emerged with investigations of consumer behaviour, becoming evident with Ernst Dichter's motivational research in the 1950s [Greenbaum 1988] and focus group applications to marketing research by Lazarsfeld [1972]. Since then, the field of qualitative research has grown significantly with methods being applied especially to:

- health, nutrition and population issues
- marketing and advertising
- social and cultural research

Currently, the field is still considered new and the scope for application almost untapped, especially in social science research. One of the most consistent areas of usage is in the area of marketing, but the new interest in the methodology is undoubtedly because of social marketing, that is, the need to understand behaviour and thereafter to transform awareness into appropriate behaviours. The thrust towards social marketing is closely related to developments (or absence of) in health-related research, including in the areas of contraceptives, food and nutrition, HIV/AIDS, and chronic diseases. In addition to the social marketing initiatives, qualitative techniques also represent foundation methods in Rapid Assessment Procedures (RAPs) [Scrimshaw and Gleason 1992], and Participatory Appraisal Methods (PAMs). These new approaches to data gathering encourage increased rates of data collection and access to information, as well as greater levels of interaction with intended beneficiary communities – a practice especially important in developing countries.

The nature of qualitative research

Qualitative research is not a single procedure. In fact, there are many distinct methods which could be classified as being qualitative in nature. The traditional tools – indepth interviewing and participant observation techniques – have been used by anthropologists for many years. Increased multidisciplinary approaches to problem solving have resulted in such tools being more accessible to, and accepted by, others.

Essentially, qualitative research is a data gathering technique which allows access to indepth feedback about or from subjects and situations. In a previous era, analyses of the data collected relied solely on subjective evaluations, and could be distinguished from the quantitative process by an absence of empirical measurements. In recent times, however, it has been increasingly acknowledged that computer technology, for example, has an important part to play in such analyses.

Types of qualitative research

There are several types of qualitative research, the more well-known including:

- content and narrative analyses
- document, material, and symbol analyses
- evaluation research
- field research (or participant observation)
- focus group discussions
- indepth interviews
- mapping exercises
- motivational research
- ranking exercises
- visual capture (photography)

Many of these 'methods' represent activities conducted on a daily basis by researchers and non-researchers alike – but without being recognized and appreciated as elements of a formal research methodology.

There are other aspects of research which are qualitative in nature, and which relate to basic field techniques inherent to the survey process:

- gaining entry, and becoming involved in field situations
- making introductions
- developing and maintaining rapport
- gaining acceptance

Some of these might seem quite similar, not only to each other, but to other methods. Differences will be highlighted in this chapter.

One of the great advantages of qualitative research is the insight into attitudes, behaviour, and motivation which it affords investigators. The types of details accessed through this methodology are very difficult to imagine and, moreso, to achieve, through any other research methodologies. It is for this reason that the methods are being adapted to research in the field of social sciences.

Advantages and disadvantages of qualitative research

There are both advantages and disadvantages to qualitative research. Recognition of the advantages has been responsible for increased utilization of the methods. The disadvantages have undoubtedly fuelled the validity debate and have been responsible as well for restricted use of the approach to date. Some of the considerations are indicated in Box 5.1.

BOX 5:1	ADVANTAGES
Advantages and disadvantages of qualitative research	

ADVANTAGES

Qualitative research

- ○ allows for indepth assessment of issues being researched
- ○ allows for investigation of highly sensitive issues
- ○ allows for comprehensive subjective evaluation based on interpersonal interaction over an extended period
- ○ can be moderated regarding location, schedule, content, pace and continuity, therefore allows flexibility
- ○ can be applied to a number of fields of investigation
- ○ can stand on its own and form complete data gathering techniques, or can be used at different phases of investigation
- ○ allows for concurrent 'observation' by interested parties with input where applicable
- ○ can often be implemented without multiple human resources
- ○ can offer particularly keen insight to the single researcher since he or she can be involved in all phases of method

DISADVANTAGES

Qualitative research

- ○ relies primarily on subjective assessments in data collection phase
- ○ allows limited extrapolation to the general population
- ○ utilizes much smaller 'sample' units than quantitative techniques
- ○ seems deceptively easy to organize, implement, analyse and report
- ○ can be easily misused, misunderstood, due to relative naturalness of methods
- ○ can be costly on a per capita basis
- ○ has a relative lack of formal theoretical and operational guidelines, which limits the respectability afforded its methods
- ○ is not yet well known and/or accepted as a bona fide, formal research technique by the wider scientific community

The qualitative versus quantitative debate

The concept of comparative assessment has also been influential in the debate regarding the virtues of qualitative versus quantitative methods of research. Importantly, it is the end to which the method is being applied which needs to drive the process used, for example 'What are the objectives of study?' There are some basic and important differences between the two approaches.

Qualitative research

- cannot provide information about frequencies of occurrence, prevalence, and so on. That is, it cannot answer the questions: 'How much?', 'How many?', or 'How often?'; these need to be answered by quantitative research
- is not normative, and is not designed to provide information about absolute trends within the population, but instead to provide indepth reports on individuals, small groups, and/or situations from or in which population subjects are likely to be represented

Introduction to Social Research

- does not utilize highly structured schedules, for example questionnaires for data collection
- relies on semi-structured and unstructured approaches to fieldwork, which allow for the depth of information made available, and cater to the spontaneity inherent in researcher, participants, and situations
- is flexible beyond the start of the process, with the possibility for making and incorporating changes into the data collection process, analyses and reporting formats, while retaining the ability to provide complete and accurate outcome indicators
- relies on words

Quantitative research

- is based on norms within a given population, and the method assesses, predicts and reports on such indicators using statistical analyses related mainly to rules of probability
- is a labour intensive method, requiring much human input in different phases of implementation
- is relatively inflexible after the process has been initiated, with limited options for change in structure, form, components, methodology, and so on
- requires a structured scientific approach to design, data collection, analyses, and reporting, with limited acceptability of artistic or literary fluency
- relies on numbers

There is still much left to the debate, and it will continue for some time to come. This is because qualitative research is still in a state of infancy. Regardless of the state of the discussions, qualitative research methods are being used and slowly developed as the need for such indepth information increases.

Qualitative Research Procedures

The actual process of conducting qualitative research is one which eventually becomes easy – or rather, natural – as the researcher becomes more skilled. One of the features of development includes the awareness that each experience, for example, each focus group is a new entity, with combined factors never being experienced in any other group. Therefore, the researcher's objectivity must *always* be maintained.

Qualitative research borders on the premises and practices of psycho-therapy, counselling and social work procedures. One major difference is the relative inability of the researcher to heal and/or take interventive action and/or offer therapeutic remedies. The intimate situations in which the researcher is involved with the subject/participant sometimes precipitate cathartic situations. It is a field in which 'sensitivity', 'sympathy' and 'empathy' are key to encouraging disclosures.

Some procedural assumptions
In approaching qualitative processes, there are a few factors *must* be assumed:

- Much of the research involves *interacting with people*, and doing so in subjective situations, so the researcher has to be understanding, able to communicate effectively, showing empathy where necessary, yet be guided primarily by objectivity.
- Flexibility is an intrinsic part of the process, but has to be used judiciously and be strictly monitored.
- In order to stand by the process and justify the outcome, there has to be a *systematic* approach to investigation, measurement, and analysis.

It is very important that socially oriented research using these methods be as deliberate and well defined as possible. Such precautions would assist in enforcing the objective nature of the process, and maintaining the rigour and integrity of the process. Methodologies need to be:

- justifiably conceptualized
- reasonably operationalized
- strictly applied

with

- adequate 'sampling'
- rigorous data collection
- keen attention to data analysis
- considered data interpretation
- clear reporting

The Basic Research Processes

There are several stages involved in any research process. They begin with the formulation of questions and end with some interpretation and report on the answers to those questions. Following these stages is also important for qualitative research. Table 5.1 highlights the options involved in the stages:

Table 5.1   Stages in the research process

Stage 1	What do I want to investigate?
Stage 2	Why do I want to conduct such an investigation?
Stage 3	What do I know about the topic for investigation?
Stage 4	What work has already been done in the area?
Stage 5	What theories have been put forward regarding the key issues?
Stage 6	How does the work that has already been done influence my thoughts on the topic and related issues?
Stage 7	How am I going to formulate the questions for investigation in light of what I now know about the topic?
Stage 8	What methodology am I going to use to answer these questions?
Stage 9	How am I going to define, operationalize and measure the variables?
Stage 10	What sampling frame am I going to use, and how will I choose my sample?
Stage 11	How will the data be collected and the process supervised?
Stage 12	How will the data be collated, edited, and coded?
Stage 13	How should the data be prepared for analysis?

Stage 14	Having prepared the data for analysis, what methods will be used to analyse the data?
Stage 15	What are the key variables being used in the analysis?
Stage 16	How shall I interpret the data?
Stage 17	How will I report on the findings from the study?
Stage 18	How does the study data report on and answer the research objectives, and relate to previous findings on the topic?

Qualitative research in the Caribbean

The Caribbean has not necessarily lagged behind in the use of qualitative methods – not any more than other developing or developed regions. There are many studies which have been conducted using these techniques, for example in communication, contraception, environmental health, food and nutrition, HIV/AIDS, public health, and sexuality studies. Many others are being designed and will be implemented in these and other fields. At the same time, there has been no structured and/or systematic attempt to forge ahead with the development of these methods and thereby increase the range of topic areas to be addressed in the region. Developing such techniques for the Caribbean poses special challenges for a number of reasons, not least being the following:

- Literacy is a problem in many countries, and the importance of this relates to word fluency, numeracy, as well as reasoning abilities.

- Caribbean societies are relatively closed, and people live in fairly close social and physical proximity to each other. This is highlighted by the importance of the oral tradition. For some of the qualitative techniques, and especially those being conducted on sensitive issues, these facts present unusual problems for impliementation and maintenance of confidentiality in such research.

- The tradition of informal community gatherings and communal knowledge makes it more difficult to structure and conduct independent, objective, qualitative research at such a level, without intervention.

- Multi-partnered relationships and parenthood heighten the tensions within small communities making many group situations rife with interpersonal tensions. These restrict cohesion and complicate data interpretation.

- Ethnicity, heritage, social class, lifestyle and political allegiance create further barriers to enactment and fluency within groups.

- The issue of access is important, with restrictions being due, for example, to telephone and media coverage, as well as to roads and transportation systems.

Such restraints complicate as well as challenge the conduct and development of qualitative research in the Caribbean.

Techniques of Qualitative Research

Three techniques will be discussed in detail. They are:

1. Basic field techniques including introductions and rapport

2. Field observation techniques

3. Depth interviewing

Basic field techniques

Most of the qualitative research methods indicated previously involve fieldwork. The researcher, or persons instructed by the researcher, is required to go into the field and gather data related to the study topic. The first stages will be regarded as simple, since they are so similar to daily life. However, the researcher in need of information must remain aware of the procedures that will result in gaining entry and acceptance into the community. Some of the essential factors related to fieldwork for qualitative research are discussed below.

New territories, suspicions and entry

The success in gaining entry into a community to conduct research is largely dependent on the first impressions of those within the community, and management of these early interactions by the researcher. Personality, appearance, and attitudinal factors are all important, and these include facial expressions; fear; contempt; respect; questions asked; response to comments; mode and features of transportation; and dress.

One of the important features in the Caribbean experience is the relative closure of communities which makes any intruder very noticeable. In situations where there is, for example, private and/or illicit activity, or where residents are outstandingly different in cultural heritage, such factors become even more important.

Subjectivity and ease of interactions

At several stages within field research, the tendency will be for the researcher to target persons with 'pleasing' expressions, including those conveying happiness, beauty, and a responsive demeanour and disposition. The reasons for this include the human fear of failure or rejection. There are pros (+) and cons (–) to the practice, which include:

(+) it might assist the researcher in becoming more comfortable

(+) the ease conveyed by the researcher could help to relax other community members

(–) it is less likely to be based on the required objective focus for study, and might set a precedent for future interactions within the situation

(–) the informant might not be a well respected and/or trusted community member, in which case any extended discussions with the researcher could jeopardize future related interactions

Prescribed (pre-scribed) roles

There are 'rules of engagement' which extend to the roles unconsciously written for individuals. Community members might make assessments of persons, situations, and possible consequences of interaction based on predetermined factors. Such factors include:

- topical interest in, or occurrences related to specific issues (e.g. cholera, HIV/AIDS)
- current societal or community, media or public relations campaigns
- previous or concurrent investigatory or research efforts in the community
- persons associated with, or accompanying the researcher into the community
- features conveyed through visual codes such as dress, transportation mode, and official signature (for example marked institution vehicle)

Also important in the recognition of roles is the need for the researcher to identify and introduce the purpose of his or her presence to the persons regarded as community leaders. Such persons could be community council or youth club leaders, caretakers, church or school leaders, political representatives, or 'Dons'. Regardless of the descriptors, recognition of their importance in the area is important, and needs to be acknowledged in the early stages.

Describing purpose and ensuring understanding

The objectives of the research project will determine how much information is conveyed during the introduction of a study to non-participants, that is, to community facilitators. The first instinct might be to 'tell all', but this might prove detrimental. Early and full disclosure of study objectives might for example, lead to:

- non-truths or half-truths by participants
- bias in selections and/or cooperation
- studied 'preparation' for participation
- unwarranted and unwanted preliminary community discussions on the study topic, leading to bias

General indicators could be as follows:

1. Provide sufficient information to ensure that:
   - accuracy of disclosures will be maintained throughout the study period
   - concerns about involvement and justification will be addressed
   - there will be minimal fears regarding validity of study or researchers
   - trust in the purpose and intentions of the study and researchers will increase during the interactive study period

2. Be keenly aware of informants' and participants' literacy and comprehension levels, and pitch the explanations accordingly.

3. Remain non-affiliated regarding political, religious, and corporate/brand persuasions and interests, as well as on any other factor which might be responsible for divisiveness between individuals or adjacent communities.

The objective focus

Despite the need to 'be' a personality in gaining entry, making introductions, and explaining the purpose of the study, it is vital for the researcher to remain objective. There needs to be an almost clinical approach to the situation –

despite the subjectivity of the interactions. This is a very difficult balance to achieve, reminiscent of survey interviewing, but critical to the success of any fieldwork.

Subject personalities and external intrusions

The persons who have been singled out for attention in a research study could be, for that period, the equivalent of 'stars' in the eyes of onlookers and those who were not selected. There will be peer and community pressure brought to bear on the individuals themselves as well as on the situations. This extends to those who might want to be onlookers and commentators.

The management of such dynamics is the responsibility of the researcher. Naturally, much care has to be exercised here, since alienation could result if the situations are not handled properly. Of special importance are inner-city and/or ghetto areas, where mismanagement could easily result in cessation of further study, since 'egos' are at stake.

Transitory functions and acquaintances

The researcher is always aware that he or she is conducting a study and will be in the area for only a restricted period of time. This may both help and hinder the communication.

First, it can assist in generating full disclosure since there is little fear of 'using the secrets within the community.

Secondly, fairly strong bonds could be formed between the researcher and individuals within the community, for example, with someone who was particularly helpful during the study. There is little likelihood of these being strengthened over time, and that fact creates some degree of mistrust regarding intent – especially towards the end of an assignment.

Thirdly, some community members might not regard accurate disclosure as being essential, since the researcher will soon be gone, and would probably not see evidence of inaccuracies or untruths.

Trust and confidentiality

The matter of enlisting and gaining community trust is of critical importance in fieldwork. The key factor to remember is that it is the researcher who wants something from the people – and they can decide to oblige or not as they will. Lack of trust might prevent participation, but gaining that trust will very likely result in cooperation. Gaining trust is dependent on many aspects of the inter-action between researcher and community members, including:

- perceived honesty
- consistency of behaviour and information provided
- the ease which the researcher is perceived to feel within the community setting
- the extent to which the researcher is perceived to appreciate and respect the community, its standards, and modus operandi
- the extent to which the study/project is seen as being of potential benefit to the community and/or its members

- whether the researcher is regarded as merely being an 'informer'
- the rapport developed between the researcher and different, respected community members

The issue of confidentiality is related to trust. Having gained trust within the community, the onus is on the researcher to maintain any confidences shared by the interactions – whether or not stated or requested. Disclosures made from such interactions, if not prudently managed, could jeopardize future research efforts within that and other communities. Further, there could be serious repercussions from unapproved disclosures.

For qualitative research, it is not only the researcher who has to maintain confidences. The interactive nature of the work means that participants may hear about each other's personal situations. This is not the case with survey research, for example, since questionnaires are administered individually, and only the interviewer knows of the responses. It is difficult but important to convey to focus group participants, that they also need to respect any confidences shared within the sessions.

For the Caribbean, making this request is very important (although the researcher cannot guarantee that it will be honoured), given the tendency for much community discussion. The researcher will never be able to monitor the participants, and disclosures could later result in interpersonal feuding within the community.

Verbal communication

To maintain the objective component of the research process, it is best to standardize dialogue used with community members and study participants. The 'standardization' is best achieved through having written guidelines to be followed at each stage, and by all those persons responsible for making disclosures about the study. The first impression would be that this would restrict the fluency and spontaneity necessary to gain entry and develop rapport. It probably will, but it must be followed for the following reasons:

- There are likely to be many persons with whom the researcher will come into contact during the stages of the study.
- On reporting the results of the study it is important to indicate what participants were told regarding, for example, the purpose and benefits of the study.
- It makes it unnecessary for the researcher to have to try and remember what different persons were told about the study.

Non-verbal communication

The last but certainly not the least important aspect relating to field techniques for qualitative research is non-verbal communication. This comprises many features, some of which have been mentioned previously. A few will be addressed in more detail.

1. *Looking and staring*: As inconsequential as this aspect might seem, it is important within a community setting. The first tendency for an outsider should be to observe (see section below on 'field observation techniques') people in their natural surroundings, make note of their

dwellings, activities, clothing and foods. This has to be done carefully since it could be misconstrued. Again, in ghetto/inner-city communities, such activities could be seen as intrusive, and in the extreme could result in harm to the researcher.

2. *Garments and colours worn*: It is important for the researcher to gain early insight into customs and traditions within the communities. Examples are the relatedness of specific colours to political affiliation in inner-city communities in Jamaica and the strength of 'rasta' colours as indicators of support for the religion.

    The researcher might be tempted to align himself or herself and wear 'orange' if working with areas supportive of one party, and 'green' when working with areas supportive of the other. *The best tactic is to avoid these colours entirely* – for if working in both areas it would be difficult to justify the alignment and gain entry.

    On working with 'roots' people, the researcher might want to indicate allegiance and get dressed in, for example, a red, gold and green belt to signify his or her own grass roots nature. This could well alienate some participants who might not be endeared to the creed of the Rastafarian movement – regardless of their basic disposition.

    In addition, the credibility of the researcher could be threatened due to subconscious application of the 'prescribed roles' mentioned earlier.

3. *Acceptance of physical environment*: There will be trying times for the researcher in the field, many of which might be related to endurance of physical conditions. These could be particularly stressful if there are socio-economic differences between researcher and participants in the community. Some of the situations which could occur are shown in Box 5.2.

BOX 5:2
Field situations requiring researcher judgement

1. *Offer of water*: to accept or not to accept?

2. *A need to use the toilet facilities*: to ask or not to ask 'if available', and for permission to use?

3. *Dirty children who want to sit on your lap*: to allow or not?

4. *Boys leaning on, and playing around your car*: to say something or not?

5. *You need to leave and go into another room*: to take your valuables or not, and if yes, how to do so and maintain 'trust'?

6. *After working in the community, you are asked for a drive*: to give or not to give?

7. *After being around the community for a while, someone makes sexual advances to you*: to encourage discussion or not, and how?

8. *Some participants want to contact you in the future – maybe for a job*: to provide contact number and/or address, or not?

There are no single answers to the above; they are judgment calls.

Field observation techniques

Field observation has its genesis in anthropology. It is an ethnographic method initiated from some philosophical framework, and involving a process of phenomenal exploration. Techniques employed in conducting field observations are no longer limited to anthropology, but are being increasingly utilized in advertising, marketing, medicine, nutrition, psychology, social work and sociology.

It could be said that 'observation' is not a research technique, but a process and product of being part of the research experience. This is not necessarily true, for a team of persons from varying backgrounds could visit a research site yet provide vastly different feedback regarding the community features observed. Good observation requires a 'readiness', which could be likened to the 'seeing eye' of an architect, artist, or designer. Some develop the techniques over time, but with technical detail rather than an intrinsic absorption being the more useful tool for analysis.

Participant versus non-participant observation

As with other methodological comparisons previously mentioned, the value of 'participant' versus 'non-participant' observation is still being debated.

Participant observation is essentially an involvement process, whereby the researcher becomes a part of the situation, with or without community members' knowledge of the purpose of such involvement. From that viewpoint, the researcher is able to 'live' the experiences of the community, thereby better understanding the customs, traditions, lifestyle and perceptions of its members.

The concept of non-participant observation has been questioned to a greater extent, on the basis that it would be very difficult for a researcher *not* to be involved in community situations if he or she was working within the environment. Nevertheless, this technique implies less involvement and disclosure regarding intent, orientation, and activities in which the researcher engages during the community study.

Observation studies can represent the whole – or a part – of the entire study to be conducted on an issue. In newly developing fields of RAPs and Participatory Rural Appraisals (PRAs), for example, observation techniques are very useful indicators for the preliminary determination of community traditions and operations, as well as for establishing the bases for future research procedures.

Applying observation procedures

Many procedures can be used for observing and understanding people's activities, personal and social situations within the community setting. These include:

1. Visiting places of community involvement:
   - shops, groceries, markets and supermarkets
   - churches and church meetings
   - community and youth centres
   - nurseries and schools
   - health centre and hospital
   - playing fields and meeting-corners

- bars or rum-shops
- work and industrial sites: hairdressing salons, barber-shops, tailoring establishments, dressmaking shops, mechanic shops, factories and offices
- farms and packaging plants
- dance-halls, local parties and community fairs

2. Identifying and holding discussions with key informants such as found in the above locations.

3. Spending extended periods (residential or otherwise) within the communities under study. The length of time is dependent on funding and resources, study objectives and methods, required outcome, and known or perceived complexity of the community. Such time periods could be for years.

Recording observations

As with other qualitative research methods, there are options for recording data from observation processes. The early decisions about the application of participant versus non-participant techniques are important in choosing recording procedures. Among the options are:

- using audio tape-recorders
- making video tape-recordings
- making handwritten notes during the observations
- making notes during the observation by using a portable (notebook) computer
- using a standard, and previously formatted schedule for concurrently recording field observations
- foregoing concurrent notes for those taken after the field sessions

Depth interviewing

Depth interviewing, or indepth interviewing, is based on the most intimate interpersonal interaction – a *dyad*. Two persons sit to discuss issues, with the knowledge and understanding that there will be complete honesty, openness, mutual trust, limited interference, minimal limitations on time, and subsequent regard for confidentiality of disclosure.

The absence of other participants makes the depth interview ideal for case studies, life history assessments, and qualitative research on sensitive issues. No other methodology is as ideally suited for collecting the detailed and sensitive information that can be collected through the depth interview (Box 5.3).

BOX 5:3 **The depth interview**	*What is a depth interview?* Pearl sat motionless in the chair. Tears trickled down her face. Her eyes begged the confidante to understand why this was happening. She had been talking about the beatings inflicted on her young daughter. Beatings which were really about her own frustration. The years of trying too hard. For too little reward. The unending misery of her existence. And not knowing what her options were. She didn't even have anybody to talk to. Now her

Introduction to Social Research

children were grown. And the same daughter was unkind to her children. Not taking care of them as a mother should. Not even trying. She was too interested in parties, and men. The same men who were making her pregnant then leaving. What could she do to change the situation?

The lady is taking part in a depth interview. And the discussion had led her into the past realities of her life. Made her remember what she had managed to forget for so long. She had just decided not to focus on these painful aspects of life. Now she remembers and she talks about it.

Concepts in structuring depth interviews

The depth interview utilizes a semi-structured guide, similar to that used for focus groups, but even less structured. What is important is the formatting and statement of *issues* related to the areas of interest and objectives of study.

Generating the flow within the dyad is difficult but important. Key concepts and roles of the interviewer, and those which create and maintain the momentum, include:

- encouraging trust
- generating and encouraging feedback through probing (see chapter 7 on 'Data Collection Methods for Surveys') and non-verbal communication
- listening

Limiting intrusions and using support materials are sometimes important for successful application of this method, given the intensities of the situation. The problems of literacy can restrict the use of written support materials. However, pictorial representation could be useful.

Identifying and recruiting participants for depth interviews

This process must be driven by the study objectives. The research project will have been centred around particular themes, with identification of subjects to be studied, for example, 'from a specific television target audience', 'product/service users', 'diabetic women', 'pregnant women', 'male factory workers'. These will be the first descriptors used in identifying the communities from which the respondents are to be drawn.

It might be necessary to develop a screening questionnaire if:

1. The participants (interviewees) are to be chosen from a large cadre of potential respondents; and/or
2. If there are many criteria which have to be satisfied by the respondents.

It is important to remember that among the basic tenets of qualitative research are the stated non-representativeness of the 'sample' of cases or respondents, and the inability to generalize from the research findings to the general population. Therefore, it is not necessary to fulfil any expectation of full representativeness. The process is aided by the willingness of the respondents to participate in the study.

Full disclosure of interview content is neither required nor possible, but the prospective respondents should be provided with sufficient information to allow them to make an informed decision regarding participation.

Cautions and difficulties related to depth interviewing

One of the main problems encountered during depth interviewing is the conflicting role of the interviewer. Given the use of this research method for investigating lifetime and sensitive issues, it is almost predetermined that there will be painful situations recounted. The types of topics which can generate such difficult situations include:

- poverty, its effects on the interviewee and household members, and its realization and disclosure
- adult or childhood abuse (emotional, mental, physical, and sexual) – even if not recognized as 'abuse' during the experience
- experiences involving extreme hardship
- situations involving disregard and/or disrespect and/or disloyalty to or for, the individual

The interviewer, however, is not there as psychotherapist or psychiatrist, but to collect information. Among the more humane solutions to this problem is the establishment and use of a referral system, geared towards those respondents who request assistance for problem solving.

Main Points

📖 Qualitative research is an approach comprising several methods and applications, for example, indepth interviewing, focus groups, observation techniques, mapping and visual capture.

📖 The approach has been used in anthropology for years, but new methods are increasingly being added to older ones and applied to public health issues, in attempts to effect behavioural changes.

📖 This type of research is based on subjective, personal and experiential situations, only some of which are highly structured. In addition, growth and development of some qualitative methods has been limited, more attention being given instead to their applications.

📖 Advantages of qualitative research include indepth investigation, data gathering into sensitive issues, flexibility of application and involvement of primary researcher. Disadvantages include the subjectivity of assessments, limited extrapolation to the general population, apparent ease in implementation and therefore likelihood of abuse, and limited acceptance by the wider scientific community.

📖 There are some factors which should be given special consideration in using qualitative techniques in the Caribbean, for example, low literacy levels, closed communities, a tradition of having informal gatherings, and the range of backgrounds which limit fluency in group situations.

📖 The researcher's approach to, and presentation of self within, the community and to individuals themselves, for example, when conducting indepth interviews, is very important in gaining acceptance, and achieving good study results. This process includes consideration of roles, suspicions, description of purpose, trust and confidentiality issues, verbal and non-verbal communication, and the need to maintain an objective focus.

Exercise

Working in groups of approximately four persons each, describe study outlines (one per group) which would involve investigation in **one** of the following types of community: church, hospital, marketplace, school. The descriptions must include study objectives, and a brief methodology which would involve conducting observations.

Based on the study objectives identified, design a short, relevant list of features to be observed in the respective communities; for example, physical layout, structures and utilization, types of people and the descriptors used in classification, interactions between people and perceived relationships based on age and gender. Prepare for community visits by discussing logistical details such as times for visiting, types and details of disclosure to be made, and recording format appropriate to your study. Each person within each group should conduct their observations independently, but simultaneously with other group members.

Briefly report results from the observations by comparing findings within the group based on study objectives. Any changes made to methods in order to facilitate the study should also be discussed. If more than one group conducted a study in a similar community, compare types of observations made within that type of community.

Chapter Six | Focus Groups Techniques[1]

Focus groups represent another type of qualitative research method. This fact may not yet be generally accepted, but reasons have been given for their inclusion in the category [Morgan 1988]. They are extremely versatile in application, and in many instances are a cumulative representation of the methods outlined for the other qualitative approaches to investigation. Focus groups can be and are used in a variety of disciplines and settings, including advertising, anthropology, education, food and nutrition, marketing, sociology, population, and psychology.

In general, a focus group can be described (see Box 6.1) as:

> . . . a fairly homogeneous group of persons who come together to discuss a particular topic, based on a topic guide, and with guidance from a moderator, effecting results which benefit from the group interaction . . . The strength of a focus group discussion is due to the interaction of

participants in a *non-threatening environment*, based on *mutual interest and trust*, and stimulated both by *interest in the topic* and the comfort of *discussion with peers*.

The apparent simplicity of the method arises mainly because of the resemblance to "a group of friends sitting around and talking". This definition unfortunately belies the intensity of the operations involved in constructing, administering, analysing and reporting on, the set of groups in any focus group study.

Nevertheless, the fact that effective management of a focus group study can generate the fluency required to give that impression, would be a credit to the principal researcher for such a study.

<table>
<tr><td>

BOX 6:1
The focus group session

</td><td>

What are focus groups about?

Imagine a group of about eight persons sitting in a room. The atmosphere is intense, and there is deep concentration amongst the participants. They are parents discussing "the influence of media on children's development". They are talking about television now. Violence. Sex. Drugs. Abuse of power. Entertainment. Fashion. News. Some mothers are angry about the decline in values and the corruption in societal behaviours which are surely taking place because of television. Other parents, mostly the fathers, are less concerned about this issue, and feel that moral decay would have been evident even without television. What is important to them is that their children have learned about world views and what technological developments have been taking place in Japan. Their own children have become more aware of environmental issues such as conservation and recycling options. They have also seen starvation and hopelessness in Ethiopia, and the consequences of war throughout the world. There is one man who is not saying much at this point. The discussion has energies of its own. He is intent on listening to what is being said, and the passion being conveyed on the respective issues. This man looks on – from one person to the next, watching the anger. Feeling the heat of debate. But there are two participants who have to be monitored. One is speaking too much, and the other hardly at all. The man glances at a document in front of him. And he glances at the clock. The discussion has to be led into a more detailed treatise of 'interpersonal violence' and 'sex'. These are key issues which have been stated in the project objectives and which still have to be covered before the group disbands.

These persons are *focus group participants* – both mothers and fathers. The man guiding the discussion is the *moderator*. The document at which he is looking is the *topic guide*.

Analysis of interaction: Some of the factors and dynamics of which focus groups are comprised include:

- accuracy – probing for, and verification of consistency
- communication skills – monitoring conversation/interaction/ feedback and retaining in memory

</td></tr>
</table>

- applying essential interviewing methods
- completeness – comprehensiveness including depth and range at individual and group levels
- confidences – reassuring and maintaining confidentiality
- environment – monitoring atmosphere within – and outside – the group
- information – discussing issues and ideas
- uncovering attitudes and opinions
- intimacy – one factor encouraging participation and disclosure
- personalities – multiplicity within, to be incorporated and monitored.

The group situation: Unlike the indepth interview or the survey, the success and 'rhythm' of focus groups are based on sustained interaction between individuals comprising a group. These individuals are usually unknown to each other prior to the group situation.

Focus groups represent one of the few research methods where participants are encouraged to interact with each other. Contrary to other methods which discourage such communication, focus group sessions largely depend on this interaction. The exact number of participants in focus groups varies from project to project, as well as from one group to the next. In the past, most groups were conducted with ten to twelve persons. The accepted numbers have decreased over the years, but the current thinking is that eight persons represent the ideal group.

The moderator: Although it is the interaction of the participants which will determine the quality of a particular session, the discussion is led by a 'moderator'. The moderator is a trained professional whose role is multifaceted and includes directing the 'flow' of the discussion. The moderator's role seems deceptively simple, although one of the most likely errors in the function is to engage participants in a 'question and answer' session.

Other factors for which the moderator is responsible include ensuring the inclusion and minimum participation of all persons in the group and ensuring that all related study objectives are met in the session.

The topic guide: The group discussion is focused on particular issues which are outlined in a 'topic guide', 'discussion guide', 'focus group outline', 'schedule' or 'protocol', the designing of which is closely linked with the study objectives.

This document is the equivalent of the 'questionnaire' in quantitative research. However, in focus groups, the questions are open-ended and less structured, sometimes including support materials, and with a format designed to encourage the natural flow and discussion of issues.

The Attraction of Focus Groups

Focus groups have now become the vogue and there are a number of reasons for this new interest:

1. They allow for more indepth assessments of factors related to the phenomenon under study, than could be obtained through surveys

2. They require significantly less labour intensive input than do surveys, especially at the fieldwork level.

3. The per capita unit costs for administration are less than for indepth interviews.

4. They are versatile in their administration, with respect to procedures, locations, and use of supporting stimulus materials.

5. The results can be accessed in a shorter period of time than for surveys.

6. They can contribute much to baseline data collection and review, programme evaluation, information, education and communication (IEC) strategy development, as well as to policy development.

7. The procedures and skills are readily transferable to a number of disciplines and problem-solving requirements.

The use of focus groups in the Caribbean has increased significantly in recent years. The methodology allows for effective information dissemination from a 'bottom-up' perspective, the process of data gathering benefiting substantially from the sharing, community spirit of the Caribbean peoples. Problems with limited literacy can also be largely overcome through use of this method, while still gathering valid data for research purposes.

Regional interest in this participatory methodology has been fuelled by its suitability in formally harnessing small group discussions in countries known to favour oral communication. It is therefore relatively easy to engage participants in meaningful discussion for purposes of investigation, and this has been done successfully in areas and on issues such as:

- Advertising
- Agriculture
- Communication
- Culture
- Food and Nutrition
- Health
- Human Resources
- Marketing
- Sexuality
- Violence

Implementation and interpretation are not always given sufficient priority, however, and it is therefore with accuracy and rigour that regional qualitative researchers must be concerned. Tendencies towards relaxed standards are unfortunately strengthened by many factors such as inadequate resources, limited availability of trained personnel, unresolved difficulties in appropriately recruiting participants, limiting moderator skills, and inadequate attention to data analysis. Such problems place the methodology at risk of corruption and jeopardize the integrity of the method.

How are focus groups used?

One of the great strengths of focus groups is in hypothesis generation. The group sessions can be used very effectively to explore the nature of factors which might be related to some phenomenon. They can also be used as the substantive study itself, as well as to gain further insight into findings from quantitative studies.

The use of focus groups has increased considerably for health-related research. The need to more readily attend to and effect behavioural changes for diseases such as diabetes, HIV/AIDS, hypertension, and practices such as smoking, have focused more attention on indepth analyses of human lifestyle, thereby identifying the best means of structuring IEC programmes. Social marketing, RAPs and PAMs have increased attention paid to the methods. Importantly, focus groups are also useful for situations in which there is limited literacy, for example, in some developing countries, although such benefits really accrue where there is the presence of a skilled moderator.

Some of the ways in which focus groups are used include:

- Advertising research – this is one field in which they were originally used, because of rapid turnaround to results, for example in (a) concept development and testing, and (b) storyboard and finished product testing.

- Market research – focus groups were also used for this purpose in the early stages, and remain critical in this respect to determine purchase and consumption patterns, for example (a) usage of new and old products, and (b) motivation to purchase.

- Social research – focus groups are now being much used for areas such as health, population, nutrition, lifestyle, image, and education studies, for example (a) sexuality, fertility and HIV/AIDS research, (b) school attendance and related factors, and (c) food and nutrition research.

- Programmatic research and development – for programme applications within the fields mentioned above, focus groups provide information for implementation and evaluation, for example (a) extent and determinants of knowledge and attitudes, customs and beliefs, (b) determining issues of concern, and reasons associated with them, (c) pretesting communication campaigns, for example for public relations or mass media, and (d) implications related to policy implementation.

Focus groups can provide a wealth of insight, generated by the rhythm of the group as well as the discussion topics. These sessions invite sharing of events and confidences, providing the bases on which to develop questionnaires, build public relations and advertising campaigns, as well as implement policies. Examples of verbatim comments from such sessions are shown in Box 6.2.

BOX 6:2
Verbatim comments arising in focus group discussions

DISCUSSION TOPIC:

Attitudes and behaviours related to contraceptive methods
. . . that waste matter inside for years since [your] period don't come inside will be poisoned (depo provera injectable)
. . . one woman got pregnant and the baby was born with it on its head. (IUD)

. . . if I tell him to use a condom, he have to because is my body, and I'm the
one to get pregnant (condom)

. . . body has excreta for what is produced – if vasectomy is done, body
produces semen but where is the outlet? Where does it go? (vasectomy)

. . . [taking pill in secret, and getting the man to use a condom] this is a form
of taking a stand without confrontation (contraceptive pill)

Source: Chambers and Branche [1994a]

DISCUSSION TOPIC:

Low income women and AIDS

. . . I think the condom is really the safest, most women use it when they
have more than one boyfriend. They use it with the outer ones and most
of them have sex naturally with the one you live with . . . you don't use
the condom with that one because you on protection [pill or injection]
. . . because most of them live with their boyfriend, they mostly trust that
one . . . and then again, maybe is that one going out and carry it [AIDS]
come in and give you!

Source: Chambers [1992]

DISCUSSION TOPIC:

Money and sex

. . . [women] normally look for a married man who'd give them more money
. . . (more?) . . . that's what I hear . . . less responsibility, 'cause you get
the money and you don't have to cater for food . . . you don't have to
wash . . . you not responsible for him . . . and you get the money! . . .
wherein if you have your man, you have to look after him and [then]
you get the money . . . (what do you do for this married man?) . . .
nothing . . . just take him money! . . . go to bed with him . . . for the wife
already at home – taking care . . .

Source: Chambers and Mitchell-Kernan [1993]

DISCUSSION TOPIC:

Food consumption patterns

. . . I give my little girl rice and peas and steam callaloo and when she went
to school somebody looked in the lunch kit and laughed at her . . . and
from that she doesn't want to have any lunch taken from home . . .

Source: Chambers and Branche [1994b]

What should focus groups not be used for?

Despite their obvious flexibility, there are limitations to the use of focus groups. Certain study objectives, topic areas, administrative features, and outcome measures might contraindicate their use, for example:

1. assessing quantitative issues pertaining to the individual or the
    household, for example, 'how often . . .?' or 'how many times . . .?'
    Importantly, these types of issues can still be explored within a focus
    group setting to determine the range of responses to the questions
    (thereby establishing categories for questionnaire development), and
    to identify factors influencing response;

2. results cannot be (easily) extrapolated to the population, hence usage must be restricted if, for example, prevalence rates are required;

3. extremely sensitive issues, where respondents might *not* tell the truth *because of* the group setting, thinking they might compromise their privacy; and

4. where the group is not properly composed, for example, social groups or genders are mixed where they should not be, based on the topic for discussion, resulting in a restricted flow of communication within the session.

Within the Caribbean, there are other key issues which might make use of focus groups inadvisable as the method of choice, for example:

1. sociophysical proximities – with small communities, decisions have to be made based on the subject material since 'informal, external discussions' or gossip could destroy the integrity of focus group sessions;

2. language fluency – whether the moderator and note taker are fluent in the native language, including patois and Creole;

3. reference group – the group with which the moderator and notetaker are connected, for example, the local residential community, or the Rastafarian movement, and the perceptions and profiles held by the focus group participants for these reference groups.

Focus Groups – Logistical and Developmental Issues

Effective execution of a focus group study depends on the successful combination of a number of phases. These include preparatory and executional processes for the group sessions, as well as the data management and analytical procedures required to produce a meaningful report.

Once the basic agreement to conduct focus groups has been made, one of the most difficult features of focus groups pertains to the realities and logistics of the process, for example, calculating the number of groups, coordination of groups, and actually bringing persons together for the sessions. This could be regarded as 'unfortunate' because it detracts would-be researchers from the excitement inherent in the group sessions themselves. However, it is a necessary process required to understand and appreciate the full extent of the focus group dynamics.

These logistics represent part of the 'preparation' phase within a sequence of events outlined in Box 6.3, and detailed in the following sections. The basic sequence of stages is as follows:

1. Preparation

2. Development

3. Execution

4. Data management

5. Reporting

One of the unique advantages of focus groups is the fact that the researcher can be closely involved in the process through most or all stages within the sequence as outlined above. This allows for further qualitative analyses and understanding of the results obtained. This advantage is not present in survey research, as all of the fieldwork is generally left to interviewers, who do not always relate completely the processes encountered in the field.

<table>
<tr><td>

BOX 6:3
Ten stages in conducting focus group research

</td><td>

What you need to do

A. Preparation

1. Identify and define *study details* including key issues, objectives, methods and personnel

2. Identify *procedural framework*, including any relevant ethical issues

B. Development

3. Design and develop the *recruitment screener* (optional)

4. Recruit, train and dispatch the *recruiters*

5. Design and develop the *topic guide*, with details of support materials

6. Ensure that all *field arrangements* are satisfactory

C. Execution

7. Prepare for and conduct focus group sessions, including taping, and notetaking (optional)

D. Data management

8. Prepare group summaries and/or transcriptions

9. *Review and analyse all data* (notes, tapes, transcriptions and summaries)

E. Reporting

10. Outline then prepare a *written report*; and outline then prepare an oral report (optional), and arrange for data dissemination (often done by client).

</td></tr>
</table>

Stages for Conducting Focus Groups

Each of the stages mentioned previously involves a number of additional categories. This section will outline the key features, with an emphasis on planning and procedural activities.

The 'preparation' phase

The preparation phase transforms the project proposal into an operating framework. It involves conceptualization, planning and the key factors for project management. Adequate preparations during the initial stage establish the foundation for developing, conducting, analysing and reporting on the focus groups.

Identify and define study details

The topic, problem, basic objectives and methodology will have already been identified in the project proposal. The purpose of this phase is to clarify and refine them, inclusive of procedural details.

Problem and objectives

Study objectives could be framed from additional literature reviews, after identifying 'reasons' for study from any of the following:

- a problem suggesting or representing some departure from the norm, or from data previously reported
- the need for more qualitative information about an existing situation
- the need for more detailed information with which to communicate

The objectives will identify exactly *'what the study will set out to do'*, in approximately three or four clear and concise points.

Methods

The 'methods' section in the preparatory phase will identify details of how the study will be conducted, and would include:

- *sampling and group composition* – for example, the number of groups, the key indicators for the respective groups (e.g. gender, age range, geographic location and socio-economic status), and the bases on which participants will be selected;
- *topics* – the key issues to be included in the topic guide and the format for discussions;
- *time frame and schedule for conducting groups.*

Identify procedural framework, including any relevant ethical issues

At this stage, the overall plans and schedules would be critically assessed before launching into the intensive design and fieldwork stages. The focus is on project and field management, including the total number of groups, and the composition and details for each group, for example:

- male versus female versus mixed-sex
- age ranges
- exact locations including town, physical site and so on
- time schedule including date, time
- personnel required

It is best if there is a structured format defining the composition of each group, with date, time, location, and any pertinent notes for each group session. An example is shown in Table 6.1.

The ethics issue

It is important to identify any ethical issues which might need to be considered, and obtain necessary clearance before commencing the study, for example:

- whether parental permission is required due to participants' ages, and content of issues to be discussed
- whether contents for taste testing need to be disclosed prior to group session and whether the researcher needs to get written permission from participants to guarantee indemnity
- whether it is permissible to hold sessions with children in school without receiving prior permission from parents and teachers or the Ministry of Education

TABLE 6.1 An organizational format for planning focus groups

DATE/DAY	TIME	GEOGRAPHIC DESCRIPTION		SEX		AGE RANGE (year)			MODERATOR	NOTES
		AREA	LOCATION	MALE	FEMALE	15–19	20–35	36–50		
Jan 18 /Tues	3:30pm	Urban	Moretown (School)	X		X			JB	
Jan 18 /Tues	5:30pm	Urban	Cabview (school)		X		X		HA	
Jan 20 /Thurs	6:00pm	Urban	Border (Church)	X	X			X	RM	choir at 8:00pm
Jan 22 /Sat	10:00am	Rural	Myer Cove (C/Ctre)	X			X		HA	need batteries
Jan 22 /Sat	2:00pm	Rural	Bellas (School)		X	X			JB	caretaker Mr James
Jan 24 /Mon	4:00pm	Rural	Wells (School)		X			X	RM	
Jan 26 /Wed	3:00pm	Urban	Dontown (C/Ctre)		X	X			HA	Leave by nightfall
Jan 28 /Fri	4:30pm	Rural	Pt. Lodge (School)	X	X			X	JB	

The development phase

Having defined the basic outline for the project in general, and the focus groups in particular, more details can now be added to develop the focus groups.

Design and develop the recruitment screener

The use of a recruitment screener is optional, and is usually required for studies in which the screening process might be somewhat difficult because of some specific combination of requirements. Such an instrument allows for early and precise identification of participant attributes, thereby answering the question: 'Are you qualified to participate in this study?'

Essentially, the recruitment screener (or screening guide) is important because of the need to try and organize *homogeneous* focus groups. This 'homogeneity' however, can be based on any type, and/or number of factors; some of the questions which would help to determine the need for a screener, as well as group composition, include:

- Who do you need to talk to? Why? Are they men? Women?

- What characteristics (personal/situational/working life, product usage etc.) must the participants have?
- What age should/should they not be? Why? Why not?

The recruitment screener is a questionnaire, and is constructed as indicated in chapter 8 on 'Elements in Designing a Questionnaire'. Questions will vary by project and issues, with attention to selection criteria.

In the recruitment process, participants have to be told of the exact date, day, and time for the session to which they are being invited. There should also be an exchange of contact data (for example, office number and contact name) in the event that they find they cannot attend the session, or the session is postponed. The latter should be made known whether or not there is a screener.

Recruit, train and dispatch the recruiters

The recruiting process is a very important one, with many similarities to survey interviewing. Recruiters often represent the initial link between the researchers and the prospective participants. They must therefore present the project in a manner which will encourage participation, but not divulge too much preliminary information to the prospective participants.

Reasons for providing only limited information to the prospective participant at this stage include the likelihood of:

- reduced interest
- bias towards or against the topic for discussion
- preparatory 'study' before the group session

The role of recruiters includes:

- identification and selection of suitable participants based on the agreed selection criteria (including use of screener if applicable)
- introduction of the study concept and key components to the prospective participants
- encouraging cooperation with the study, inclusive of timely attendance at the prescribed session

The process of recruiting is difficult, but extremely critical. The adequacy of choosing participants will largely determine the validity of the focus group results. The identification and recruitment of participants should not be haphazardly done if faith is to be placed in the results. This is particularly true for studies with more of a social content where the screening/recruiting procedures are likely to be more stringent.

Another issue for consideration is the question of when to recruit?. Much will depend on the exact descriptors of the group, and the knowledge that some flexibility is required in answering this question. Considerations include:

- Communication systems – it is usually much easier, and more cost-efficient to recruit by telephone, but this depends on the services available in the country.
- Occupation (general) – the types of occupations in which prospective participants will be employed are important. Housewives in a rural area, for example, could be recruited just before the sessions. Business executives, on the other hand, have less available time and should be recruited early and given constant reminders.

- Flexible schedule – the overall schedule for recruiting has to allow for flexibility. Many urban participants are only available in the evening or at night, or on weekends.

Despite the eagerness which will be inherent in the recruiting process, there are certain factors which might preclude prospective participants from being chosen for a focus group session. Some of those who would best *not* be recruited include:

- the individual whose personality is too 'strong' or too 'weak'; too opinionated, strongly biased, too loud, too boisterous; too timid, too shy, not willing to talk

The following persons will be very difficult to handle within a group situation:

- persons who have absolutely *no* interest, or too much interest, in being involved and/or attending
- persons who have had too much exposure to focus groups, and who might be 'skilled' participants

Design and develop the topic guide

The topic guide (Box 6.4) represents the equivalent of the questionnaire in survey research, presenting open-ended questions in the form of a guideline for discussion topics. Design of this instrument varies in complexity according to the study being conducted, but could be approximately two to five pages in length, identifying:

- issues for special attention
- those areas to be further probed
- how and when support materials should be used
- timing for the subsections within the guide

<table>
<tr><td>

**BOX 6:4
An outline and key features for the 'topic guide'**

</td><td>

Alcohol Consumption in the Caribbean

(a) Moderator's Topic Guide
General Introduction (b) [15 minutes]
(c)Hello, my name is _____(d)_____, and this is a (e) focus group discussion. First of all, let us introduce ourselves, by saying first names only (f). Today, we are going to talk about 'alcohol consumption' (g). The session will last for approximately 1½ hours (h).

Subject introduction (i):

○ What comes to mind when you think of the word 'alcohol'? Probe: strength, types of drinks.

○ Is there any particular time of day or week when alcohol is consumed? What are the reasons?

○ Do any type of people come to mind when you think of alcohol? how would you describe them?

Consumption patterns of family and friends (j):

○ What about your family and friends? Do any of them drink alcohol?

○ How do you feel about them drinking?

</td></tr>
</table>

BOX 6.4
cont'd

○ Are any of these people close family members or friends? What effect do you think this has had? Probe: illness, accidents, state of being drunk, effects on family and friends, and on lifestyle.

Personal alcohol consumption (k):

○ What about you? Do you drink alcohol? What type of alcoholic drinks do you mainly have?

○ How does alcohol make you feel? What does it make you do?

○ How do you feel after drinking? Probe: immediately after, morning after etc.

○ When do you mainly drink alcohol? Is there any particular reason why these times are important?

○ Who or what would you say mostly influences your drinking pattern?

Closure (l):

○ Well, we have now come to the end. Is there anything else that you thought we were going to discuss, and that you think would be important if we are talking about alcohol consumption?

Analyses

(a) The title of the study, or abbreviated title is included here.

(b) The topic guide is sectionalized, to facilitate the discussion and the moderator.

(c) Times are allocated to the different sections, so that the moderator can maintain the schedule. The total time for the session should be between $1\frac{1}{2}$ and 2 hours.

(d) The moderator introduces himself or herself, and the notetaker if one is present, and affiliation regarding the project.

(e) An introduction to the *concept* of focus groups is needed, inclusive of the number of persons, what is expected of the group regarding the discussion format, the recording method, refreshments and restroom facilities and procedures.

(f) First names are generally used to make the situation more familiar, yet still relatively anonymous.

(g) The topic and some idea of the scope of discussion are outlined here.

(h) The estimated time for the discussion is indicated, although this should also have been done during the recruitment phase.

(i) The section which initiates discussion on the subject area is designed to put the participants at ease and not feel too threatened by the persons who will hear their disclosures.

(j) By moving into issues related to *others,* the topic draws closer to self, but still not so close that the participants will not be free in their discussion.

(k) The more personal references and discussions are often left to the latter phase of discussion, especially for more sensitive topics such as in this focus group.

(l) It is important to close the discussion, and using this type of closure allows the participants to make further input into the discussion, with issues initiated by them.

It is almost impossible to expect that the original outline will be the final version, and that used for each group. There will be the need for modifications to reflect new information from early groups. Additionally, the guide should be developed in collaboration with the client to ensure that all stated objectives are being met.

Support materials

Despite the fact that the topic guide is the primary document for use during focus group discussions, it is often useful to have supporting materials and agendas, for example, background questionnaires, product samples, photographs or concept cards, psychological tests. These might be used for different reasons, including:

- forming the basis for discussion (e.g. advertising research, product development research)
- assisting in the flow of the discussion (including sensitive issues)
- dramatizing situations
- obtaining personal information/perspectives from the participants (e.g. background questionnaire/rating sheets)

Ensure that all field arrangements are satisfactory

It is *very important* to monitor the fieldwork, including recruiting, arrangements for locations, and the confirmed availability of participants. Aspects to be monitored include:

- checking completed *recruitment screeners* while recruiting is in progress, so that any problems can be corrected early
- checking *adequacy of locations,* especially those that are far away, for example time schedule, availability and suitability (noise levels/opening hours and so on), availability of refreshments, and of electrical supply for recording equipment
- *confirming* the group session with prospective participants on the day before (or same day)

The execution phase

Having made all the preliminary arrangements for the groups, the next phase is the execution.

Prepare for and conduct the focus group sessions

At the appointed time when the groups will be conducted, the following key persons should be in place:

- moderator
- group assistant who will welcome the participants, make them comfortable, assist in completing background questionnaire if necessary, prepare refreshments, and (maybe) take notes of the session
- notetaker, if different from the assistant
- participants
- client/observer (if prior arrangements have been made for unobtrusive 'observation' of the sessions)

It is best if the moderator *not* play the role of host at this time, since the dynamics of that preliminary interaction might detract from the later role to be assumed in the focus group.

If it has been decided that a notetaker will be present, this person should be familiar with the topic and issues for discussion. This will assist him or her in being better able to follow the discussion as it progresses. There should also be pre-arranged guidelines for recording notes.

The moderator might also make brief notes during the group session, but these should not be excessive, as the process of recording would detract from his or her primary role.

The seating arrangement is also of great importance in the conduct of the sessions. The aim should be to *maximize communication* (both verbal and non-verbal) between participants, and with the moderator. To do this effectively, there should be few inhibitors to the process. The use of a table for example, represents another factor in the communication equation. It is therefore optional, and use would depend on whether it is required, for example, for writing or product display.

Some of the locations available within the Caribbean setting for use as focus group locations require manoeuvring to create the best environment. Primary schools, for example, often have small chairs attached to (small) desks. This reduces the extent to which they can be moved around and made comfortable for a discussion among adults.

The data management phase

Data management includes a number of phases, some of which are dependent on the recording of data. First, it is useful to review the different options for data collection/management (see Table 6.2).

It is also possible to use multiple options for recording sessions, but this decision will depend on the specific details of the study. Once the 'recording' decisions have been made, attention can then be focused on the actual management of the data.

Prepare group summaries and/or transcriptions

One option for recording (Table 6.2) is the preparation of summaries from each session. Ideally, these should be prepared by the group moderator, with any or all session notes, as well as the tape recordings. Where this is done, it is best to have each completed soon after the session has been conducted, say within 24 hours, and *definitely* before the moderator's next focus group.

Table 6.2 Options for focus group data collection/management

METHOD	ADVANTAGE	DISADVANTAGE	IDEAL USE
Audio Tape Recording	• permanent record of session made available • important for recall of voice tone, degree of feelings, strength of group response, etc.	• unable to capture some non-verbal communication • extra caution must be exercised with equipment if recording solely dependent on this method	• all types of focus groups
Video Tape Recording	• for clients wanting to, but unable to view sessions • captures non-verbal communication, e.g. facial expressions	• more costly option • difficult to use for some rural groups, so limits consistency for some projects	• for projects where visual feedback important, e.g. consumer use of products, presentation of new ideas
Notes Taken by Notetaker	• immediate record of discussion • an independent source of feedback to supplement moderator's perceptions	• an extra 'outside' person in the group, so introduces other limitations in discussion	• for projects requiring immediate reporting
Notes Taken by Moderator	• moderator able to record immediate perceptions of session including moods, denials, etc., as well as able to further direct the discussion	• splits concentration between flow of discussion, questions, and recording	• very skilled moderator • limited immediate availability of other recorded information, e.g. from a notetaker
Session Summaries	• represents a fairly complete and accessible caption of the group session • provides opportunity for moderator to reflect on session and identify key findings • ideal for non-computerized analyses, where several summaries can represent important guide for report	• ideally has to be completed very soon after the session • has to be done by the moderator • difficult to complete adequately if many sessions are being conducted by the same moderator within a short period	• for fairly detailed reports, not requiring full verbatim transcriptions • for social types of issues
Transcription of Audio Tapes	• can be partial or full • only source for full written record of sessions • very good for detailed analysis of project group sessions • beneficial for projects where there might be follow-up work (similar/related areas) • provides raw data for computerized analyses	• very costly in terms of time, energy, and project dollars	• for projects requiring verbatim comments for IEC requirements, e.g. advertising copy, public education programmes • if report being prepared long after group sessions • if there are many sessions in project

The summaries should be approximately five pages in length, each page generally requiring about 30 minutes for completion. All important aspects of the group session would be included here, for example, highlights of sections in the topic guide, majority/minority perspectives, group composition, and group atmosphere.

Review/analyse all data (notes, tapes, transcriptions, summaries)

The concept of analysing qualitative data, is quite a difficult concept to grasp. There are few numbers to analyse, and results really represent an 'exercise in comprehension'. The approach to this type of analysis includes the following assessments:

- by group type/location/age/gender/socio-economic status
- by issue
- by study objectives

The decision regarding tools and format used for this type of data analysis is largely a personal issue, and will change with experience, but the following must be considered:

- the available results have to be reviewed by the person preparing the report
- if there are full transcriptions, then it may not be necessary to listen to the tapes
- listening to tapes is (still) important if the report writer is unsure, for example, of participants' strength of conviction based on the issues, or needs to get 'the feel' of a particular group, or if he or she was not the moderator for a particular group

The above are then incorporated for analysis into a 'long hand' version, relying on coding and tabulation principles. There are, however, more sophisticated approaches to analysing qualitative data, for example, use of computer applications, principles for which originate in anthropology. The basis on which analyses operate is 'content analysis', addressed elsewhere in this book (see chapter 9 on Unobtrusive Research). Notes that pertain specifically to use of this concept in the focus group analysis include the following:

- a full transcription of the sessions is ideally required, but a partial transcription can suffice in some cases
- the 'study objectives' generally form the elements for managing and analysing the data
- key words, phrases and/or sentences are highlighted in encoding the raw data
- computer software is available (e.g. DBASE, ETHNOGRAPH, SAS, SPSS) for data management and analysis

The rationale for attempting to analyse qualitative data is undoubtedly fuelling the debate for and against qualitative and quantitative methods, and needs to be reviewed within an ideological perspective. Quests for greater acceptability within the scientific community might well be forcing a merger of methods, that is, a 'quantification' of qualitative studies. This is especially so with the more diverse applications currently being made of qualitative methods. There are a number of essential elements to be considered here, including:

1. pressure for qualitative research to conform to traditional quantitative methods, at least in the analysis and reporting of data

2. a perceived need for technological advances to be applied in this field: achieving this application could simplify and streamline laborious, unsystematic procedures currently used in producing results from qualitative studies such as focus groups

3. many qualitative researchers feel a need to include some structured quantitative aspects in their research agenda to validate the process, for example, background questionnaires, sampling methodologies and rating instruments

The reporting phase

Whatever the data analysis methods, reporting must follow, and this phase comprises both written, and oral reporting.

Outline then prepare written report

The written focus group report is not much different from any other report (Box 6.5). Key points of departure include:

● use of verbatim comments to illustrate the analytical point, and to 'colour' the report

● more 'words' and fewer numbers than for a statistically oriented quantitative report

BOX 6:5 **Framework for a** **written focus group** **report**	**Focus group report** The written report is the most lasting documentation of the study findings. It must be written for the audience for which it is intended. Some emphasis must be placed on the issues which are of greatest importance to the client (with reference to the objectives of the study and the purpose for which the report will be used). *Cover page* – indicating the title of the report, the person or organization to which it is being submitted, the person or organization submitting, and the date of submission. *Executive summary* – to include brief statements of background to study, methods used, key findings, main conclusions, and recommendations. *Introduction or background to study* – the reasons why the study was undertaken, with specific indication of previous situations and/or information which justify the conduct of the study. *Objectives of study* – the specific objectives for conducting the study, as noted in the proposal document. *Methodology* – the methods which were employed in conducting the study, with reference to sample frame, 'sampling methodology', recruiting procedures, topics discussed, and data management procedures.

**Box 6.5
cont'd**

Results – the findings categorized by main subject areas, analyses of the information reviewed, and with use of verbatim comments to illustrate the key points. This could be the most comprehensive section of the report. The topic guide is useful as a framework for reporting the results.

Conclusions – the extent to which the findings have answered the concerns as expressed in the study objectives.

Recommendations – the directives which will be suggested based on the study findings and main conclusions relative to the objectives for doing the study, and the likely resources available for action.

Outline then prepare oral report (optional) and arrange for data dissemination

An oral report is not always required, therefore the need must first be discussed with the client. The guidelines for preparing an *oral* report, are markedly different from that for a written report, the latter assuming an audience with more time to read. Oral reporting, however, is important for highlighting the *main* findings from the study for an audience which might have much less time to spare, and much less interest in specific details. Nevertheless, audiences are different, and the first item in an agenda for preparing an oral presentation is to determine the nature and expectations of the audience.

A clear advantage in orally presenting qualitative data such as that from focus groups is the availability of verbatim comments for illustrating the points being made. At the audience level, such colourful phrases, especially within a cultural context, provide relief in the presentation and highlight the depth of meaning for which focus groups (and other qualitative methodologies) were probably conducted in the first place.

Having reviewed 'stages' in focus group research, there are now two areas that require additional mention:

1. an introduction to the dynamics of focus group sessions

2. the moderator's role within the sessions

The Dynamics of the Focus Group Session

What takes place within a focus group session is related to group discussions – such as those used for therapeutic and/or informational purposes. There are marked differences however, based on the role of the moderator, the need to monitor and control interactions, and the structure inherent in the overall methodology. The discussion of what actually takes place in a focus group and what constitutes the 'dynamics' of a focus group session includes factors such as:

- the interaction between moderator and the respective participants
- the interaction between participants, and the resultant 'rhythm' of the group
- the complexity of interactions based on verbal and non-verbal communication; seating arrangements; meeting of personalities subject matter; physical, mental and emotional atmospheres;
- the skill of the moderator in negotiating the various inputs

Introduction to the focus group session

When participants are brought together for the first time, they need to be introduced to the focus group session (see Box 6.6). Regardless of the number of times any participant has been exposed to such an exercise, this process still has to be followed. An introduction includes:

- participants' introduction to each other, preferably using *first names*
- introduction to the purpose of the gathering
- information about 'a focus group':
  - how it operates
  - what the expectations are from the participants
  - the need to discuss issues freely
  - the moderator's role
  - taping of the session
  - assurance of confidentiality
  - time schedule
  - availability of refreshments
  - availability of and procedures related to sanitary conveniences

BOX 6:6 **Introducing members** **to a focus group session**	Hello. My name is Roberta, and this is the Institute of Investigation. We are all here to have what is known as a focus group session. A focus group is where a small group of persons come together to discuss, or focus, on a particular topic. Today, we will be talking about 'pepper'. All of us have indicated that we use pepper – in some form, and at some time. When we start the discussion, all of us will have a chance to talk a lot about pepper – our own patterns of use: when, where, with what types of food, who uses it, and who does not, who should use it and who should not, etc. Before we start, I think we should introduce ourselves. You remember that my name is Roberta. If we all introduce ourselves – by first names – then we can start getting to know each other. Pat . . . Marie . . . Ronald . . . Deborah . . . Frank . . . Dawn . . . Carol . . . Jeffrey. OK, I have all the names written down now.

Today, we expect to be here for about $1\frac{1}{2}$ hours, as everybody was told. Of course, if we really get talking, and nobody wants to leave, then we might be here for a longer time. Remember though, that I have here a number of topics which we *have* to discuss, so there are times when you might notice that I am hurrying the conversation along. That will only be because I don't want to be blamed for keeping you here too late!

You will notice that we have refreshments here. Feel free to help yourselves. Yes, Dawn? . . . Of course – there's more ice on the side table. Alright . . . the bathroom is right next door. If you need to go, just leave – we will continue talking until you get back. One more thing: you will notice we have a tape recorder on the table. That's because we need to be able to recall *everything* that was said. We might not need to know exactly who said what, but there are several groups being conducted on the same topic, and I might forget exactly which group said what, so we have to tape the sessions . . . I think that's my introduction. Now, what about you – any questions up to now? . . . No? Well, let's start!

Background to the dynamics

There are several processes which will take place in the context of the focus group. Each comment/word/phrase/question/response potentially has meaning! Together, they form the dynamics of the *verbal communication* taking place in the group.

In addition, there are *non-verbal communication messages* which form part of the group dynamics. These include actions related to:

- eye contact (e.g. looking versus not looking, staring versus furtively glancing)
- body movement (e.g. sitting forward versus backward)
- arm/hand movements
- leg positioning (e.g. crossed versus open)

In addition, the relative effects of physical factors such as seating arrangements have to be considered, as they are all important in determining the effectiveness of the group session.

Monitoring the dynamics

The moderator has to be *keenly* aware of most or all of the dynamics taking place during the session. In addition to the non-verbal communication messages, there are many aspects which have to be monitored:

- ineligibility of any or all participants (e.g. due to inadequate screening)
- individual or group comfort, involvement and interest levels, (e.g. based on flow and intensity of discussion)
- divisiveness within the group, and reasons associated (e.g. lack of homogeneity in participant characteristics)
- inaccurate, incomplete, or otherwise inadequate responses
- consistencies and/or inconsistencies in response, either within, or between groups, and the implications
- new issues and perspectives which have been presented, and which could be important for further or future discussions

The personalities

There are many different personalities which will be present within any focus group. When brought together, it is the role of the moderator to synthesize these 'individual selves' into group members. One of the most important outcomes is to get the members to speak honestly and freely. The ability to do this is partly determined by the personality of the moderator (see 'Moderator requirements'), but is improved with experience and confidence.

Despite implementing the best screening procedures, problems will arise. Some of the personalities which must be monitored, have been identified [Greenbaum 1988] as:

- the *talkative* member
- the *opinionated* member
- the *silent* member

The moderator's role

The moderator has a *key role* to play in generating and maintaining the momentum within the focus group session. He or she has responsibility for *facilitating* the interaction, and meeting the study objectives.

Good characteristics for moderators

There are certain characteristics which an effective moderator will possess, some of which might be 'natural', while others are acquired. In addition, there are roles that the moderator must play, and methods by which he or she ensures that all goes well. Factors which become most important are shown in Box 6.7.

BOX 6:7
Characteristics of good focus group moderators

- *Selfless objectivity:* A good moderator needs to realize his or her role in the focus group session is that of facilitator. In doing so, the moderator's personality must serve only to encourage comfort within the group, and to enhance the flow of discussion. The moderator's style will vary, but a primary goal must be to maintain his or her own objectivity, largely by moving into the background and allowing the participants to freely discuss the issues presented.

- *Listening, visual, and critical thinking skills:* In many groups, the generation of thoughts and ideas within the group session often progresses at a rapid pace. The moderator needs to have keen sensory development, as he or she is listening, looking, and remaining alert to all utterances and nuances – whether verbal or non-verbal – continually incorporating prior information into current feedback. Highly acute memory skills are also required to facilitate this process. The relevance of all information then has to be quickly assessed to determine future directions for the discussion.

- *Learning and comprehension skills:* The real value of such groups is realized as the moderator compares discussion points with those from other groups, and from the literature. Such information is then used to facilitate and direct other points raised within each session, while operating in the framework of the topic guide.

  Included in the skills needed for this process are elements of professed ignorance (to facilitate elaboration), as well as patience, as participants conceptualize, think through and explain their thoughts on the subject materials.

- *Creative facilitator:* To achieve the above objectives, the moderator often needs to 'negotiate' the discussion, exercising much creativity and flexibility in the approach to data gathering within the session. Among the areas in which this will become necessary, are ensuring maximum participation by all members, regardless of their personalities and/or perspectives, and reviewing discussion points previously made and/or those which might be more sensitive.

- *Empathy:* The novelty of disclosure is much enhanced by conveying the surety of an unbiased 'ear' for the discussion. A good moderator would therefore possess personality traits which would encourage participants to speak freely and truthfully, without fear of embarrassment or breach of trust.

**Box 6.7
cont'd**

- Writing skills: The moderator needs to clearly and succinctly summarize group sessions within a short report. In addition, most focus groups conducted in the Caribbean are also conducted by the primary researchers who therefore have responsibility for the preparation of written and oral reports.

Gender will become an issue with sensitive and/or gender-specific topics, for example, contraceptive use, sexually related matters, and food acquisition or preparation matters. The basic rule of thumb in such situations is to use the gender with which the participants would more easily relate – given the *topic*.

Changing moderators

There are advantages to using a single moderator throughout a single project – for example, continuity in exposure to feedback. One disadvantage, however, is habituation, and the moderator being 'too familiar' with the material. He or she might become less critical and/or less keen in monitoring feedback from later groups.

Main Points

- Focus groups can be described as being 'a fairly homogeneous group of persons who come together to discuss a particular topic, based on a topic guide, and with guidance from a moderator, effecting results which benefit from the group interaction . . . '

- Use of focus groups has increased significantly in recent times, and reasons for this include indepth assessment of issues, versatility, relatively short time to provide results, their contributions to baseline data collection, information, education and education (IEC) strategy and policy development.

- Caution should be applied in using focus groups, especially where (a) there is need for obtaining quantitative data or population prevalence rates, (b) the study is on extremely sensitive issues, (c) the groups are not properly composed, (d) there are great differences between the investigator and the study groups in such areas as language, ethnicity.

- Stages that need to be included in completing a focus group study are preparation, development, execution, data management and reporting, each of which is comprised of additional steps.

- The success of a focus group relies on a skilled moderator, whose personality ideally includes being objective, a good listener with learning and comprehension skills, empathic, and creative. During sessions, the moderator has to be keenly aware of, and monitor differing personalities to ensure fluency and representativeness of interaction in the group.

- Focus groups are an important qualitative research tool, but their potential is still largely untapped. There is much scope for developing the methodology at an academic level and increasing the relevance of the method in general, and to the Caribbean region, in particular.

Working individually, identify one research topic of current social interest which could be appropriately addressed by using focus group methods. Elaborate this by preparing title, justification and objectives. This should be approximately two pages in length.

Form working groups of approximately six persons each, and choose a single topic from the above which will be studied by the group. Develop an outline to indicate the following: number and description of groups to be recruited and conducted, important variables to be considered in making groups relatively homogeneous, a two to three page topic guide to be used in group sessions, and the time schedule for conducting groups. Design the logistics for conducting the study ensuring that individual functions such as recruiter, moderator, and notetaker are rotated for group members, each person having the opportunity to participate at different levels. Group functions would be: topic guide development, data analyses, and report preparation.

On completion of the preparatory phases, each working group should conduct their study, analyse the data, and prepare a report of approximately ten pages based on the study objectives. Each focus group session should be audio tape recorded.

Note

1. The authors wish to acknowledge the extensive experience of Claudia M. Chambers in this area.

Chapter Seven

Data Collection Methods for Surveys

The Nature of Data Collection in Surveys

There are several ways to conduct research into social and related issues, many of which have been identified elsewhere in this book. Surveys represent one such data collection method, and to date it is the most widely known, accepted and used method. Surveys are conducted regularly within the Caribbean. There are many phases to the conduct of surveys and this chapter will introduce the types of survey data collection methods generally used, and details of the interviewing process. This latter is one of the most important components in ensuring accuracy of survey findings. Elements of data management will also be introduced.

The process of *data collection* in surveys is really an attempt to conduct detailed conversations using specific formatted questions with many different individuals, after they have been located, informed of the purpose and consented to participate.

The overall conduct of a survey is quite complex, for example, sampling, data management, data analysis and reporting, involving many stages, each of which holds many possibilities for error. Such likelihood is further increased since many different persons are involved in the respective phases of the survey.

Despite these facts, data collection seems to be a deceptively simple operation to the uninitiated. In fact, the same is true even within institutions where data are collected on a regular basis. Unfortunately, the process is too often conducted without real knowledge and/or appreciation for the many intricacies which correct administration entails. This apparent simplicity probably arises and persists for many reasons, some of which are:

1. the urgent need for information to drive decision making

2. the apparent ease with which questions can be scripted

3. the ready cadre of interviewers (e.g. field staff within a government institution)

4. the fact that many individuals within the population are unseasoned respondents

5. the high level of acceptability of frequency distributions, as the end result from such surveys

6. the limited utilization of and access to such findings, which restrict opportunities for more critical assessment and development of the methods and processes

The phases of data collection

Even if the focus here is limited to the data collection phases, the following activities still need to be included in the process:

- *questionnaire design* – which includes defining the scope of the study, crafting questions to address the related issues, devising and incorporating the data management and analysis procedures, testing the instrument, and refining for adequate and consistently accurate use by interviewers in the field

- *identifying the respondents* – having been advised through the sampling process of the criteria for respondent selection, the onus is then on the interviewers to accurately identify the respondents to be interviewed

- *gaining cooperation* – the interviewer needs, through a number of processes, to introduce the concept of the survey, and thereby gain and maintain the cooperation of the chosen respondents

- *conducting the interview* – with a good questionnaire as the conversation tool, the interview is conducted, every attempt being made to ensure accuracy, consistency, and continued cooperation until completion of the interview

- *recording the interview* – the interviewer needs to accurately and completely record the responses from the respondent, thereby conveying the full text of the conversation to the researcher, and eliminating or at least minimizing the possibilities of error through misinterpretation in subsequent phases

From a review of the above, it will become evident that a great deal of responsibility for data collection is invested within the *process* of interviewing, ultimately residing with the interviewer. These only become applicable, however, *after* the production of a sound and workable questionnaire, the tool to be used by the team of field interviewers (see Chapter 8, "Elements in Designing a Questionnaire").

Types of data collection

There are three main methods by which data can be collected during a survey:

1. face-to-face
2. telephone
3. mail

These vary primarily according to the *mode* by which the questionnaires are administered. Each of the above will be reviewed briefly, with some relevant comparisons being made.

1. *Face-to-face interviewing:* This is the traditional and best known method used in the Caribbean. It also has the dubious distinction of being the most intensive method of data collection, because of the extensive fieldwork and tremendous energies involved. In most surveys, the decision to conduct face-to-face interviewing also indicates a need for the following:

- sampling specific households from discrete well established units (e.g. enumeration districts (EDs)
- recruiting, training, dispatching and supervising a team of interviewers to the chosen households to conduct the interviews
- conducting interviews with those respondents specifically chosen to represent the sample

Among the greatest advantages of face-to-face interviewing are the proximity, and the interactive nature of the process. The interviewer is provided the opportunity to closely monitor the respondent using non-verbal cues. This component is *not* present in any of the other types of interviewing.

2. *Telephone interviewing:* Telephone interviewing is little used in the Caribbean for many reasons, not least of which are the following:

- the telephone systems are not always extensive enough to allow researchers to reach the full sample, consistently omitting, for example, in Jamaica, the deep rural and poor urban areas
- the telephone is not necessarily dependable, and loss of service during an interview period would result in unwanted delay in the conduct of the study
- the technology now being used to conduct telephone interviews in the United States is computer-based, extremely complex and costly, factors which make the systems even less accessible to research projects in the Caribbean

Telephone samples are generally chosen from directories which limit the universality of the population since many numbers are unlisted. This also limits the accuracy of the sampling.

Nevertheless, this type of interviewing offers great promise, especially with respect to the ease of access, and accuracy inherent in computer-based models (CATI: Computer-Assisted Telephone Interviewing) used in capturing the data. Such systems largely eliminate the need for phases such as editing, coding, and data entry, which reduce points at which errors are consistently made in the management of data from face-to-face interviewing.

3. *Mail questionnaires:* The use of mail questionnaires in the Caribbean is also limited. The method depends on the literacy of the respondents, who would have to be able to read, write and correctly respond to the questions therein. In this respect, a significant portion of the general population would be at a disadvantage, resulting in increased errors and non-response.

The problem with non-response would not be unusual, as mail surveys traditionally have a low rate of response. Their use has been enhanced with methods such as follow-up, and mixing modes for the non-respondents (for example, by using telephone techniques for interviewing).

Also important is the fact that the mail systems are not necessarily dependable, and this would result in delays as well as non-response.

All modes mentioned above depend on the questionnaire as the basic instrument by which information is gathered, but the *design features* would vary greatly, given the fact that:

(a) for the telephone, using CATI, an interviewer would be incorporating response into a standard format to be processed immediately by the computer; and

(b) for mail surveys, there would be no interviewer, and aspects such as instructions, layout and skip patterns would have to be readily accessible to, and usable by, the respondent – whatever the level of literacy.

Elements of Interviewing

When one thinks of 'interviewing' any number of situations could be conceived. These include, but are not limited to, the fields of entertainment, human resource development and management, journalism, medicine, and research. The practices and rules are all different, being based on the range of objectives. Even in conducting research interviews, there are many different approaches which could be used – based primarily on whether the study is qualitative or quantitative in nature.

'Interviewing' within the context of surveys is much different from that of mass media and personnel recruiting, for example. Survey interviewing is very different from mass media and personnel recruiting interviewing. Mass media interviews may be used for entertainment, and personnel interviews for determining suitability of individuals for a specific task. Issues of reliability and validity are not generally central to the conduct of such interviews. Furthermore, there is considerable latitude in the range and type of questions which can be asked of the respondents, based on individual traits and characteristics.

The differences lie in the survey interviews having to be standardized, their ultimate usage being realized after the data collection process. For survey interviewing, the process is not only limited to the administration of the questionnaire, but comprises other aspects, including:

- locating the respondents
- making the introduction
- gaining cooperation
- orienting the respondents
- administering the questionnaire
- recording the responses
- completing the interview

Despite the fact that conducting an interview is thought to be extremely easy, most survey interviewers would hurriedly urge caution regarding such thoughts. The problems lie as much with the possible technicality and details of the questionnaire which could influence the interview, as with the external processes such as combining the gruelling tasks intrinsic to any type of fieldwork with those mentioned above.

The importance of questionnaire design is stressed as being essential to data collection, but the interviewing process is at least as important.

Reasons for importance of the interviewing phase

The reasons for emphasizing the importance of interviewing during the data collection process include the fact that it represents one of the primary sources of errors in the conduct of surveys [Fowler 1991]. The multifaceted nature of the task makes the process prone to errors, with three factors being responsible for overall error reduction [Fowler and Mangione 1990]:

1. good questionnaire design
2. sound training
3. close supervision

Limited attention will be given to these aspects here, with emphasis being placed instead on the administration of the interview, components of which have to be included in training and monitored during field supervision. What makes survey interviewing more troublesome is the fact that the researcher very rarely has hands-on experience and knowledge of what is taking place in the field, relying instead on faith in the interviewers, and possibly on field supervisors for feedback.

The interviewing process includes personal, social and technical skills which all have to be applied consistently for all respondents by the cadre of interviewers employed to the project. The overall process demands the involvement of interviewers as well as the researcher and/or field supervisors to achieve the accuracy and consistency which typifies good survey research.

Personal and interpersonal characteristics

In considering survey interviews, it must be remembered that the interviewers are humans first, before they represent themselves as persons with interviewing roles. This means that they bring their human characteristics to bear on whatever situation they find themselves in. The concept of training is one which attempts to regulate the extent to which such qualities are applied to the interviewing process.

The interpersonal components of interviewing relate to a need to maintain a highly controlled situation in which there is limited subjectivity and maximum objectivity being applied to the process – thereby ensuring the required standardization.

Therefore, it is not surprising that research shows the desired qualities for *obtaining* the interview as being markedly different from those required for *conducting* the interview[Brenner 1985]. Whereas the former requires more and better interpersonal skills, the latter comprises more technical ones. In fact, *it is highly likely that the very skills that might be used to obtain the interview*, for example, camaraderie, discussions on general topics, *would jeopardize the integrity of the process if applied within the question and answer session.*

The personal and interpersonal factors associated with the interviewing process extend to the following:

- personality
- appearance (e.g. dress and deportment)
- speech and mannerisms
- temperament
- tenacity
- discretion and confidentiality
- handwriting

The quality of the interaction between interviewer and respondent at every phase is likely to be instrumental in determining the overall quality of the interview, including cooperation, completion and accuracy. Some of the situational responses can be and are taught within the process of training interviewers, but many are more difficult attributes to convey, since they relate to personal and interpersonal characteristics and skills not generally regarded as being important in this field.

Regardless of the impact of specific personal characteristics, for example, age, race and gender, other aspects such as non-verbal cues and related features often have to be controlled by the interviewer within the context of the interview. These include:

- smiling or laughing
- frowning
- raising the voice in irritation
- shuffling the questionnaire or other papers
- shuffling the feet or other body parts to indicate impatience or displeasure
- making encouraging or discouraging sounds
- sighing

Getting the interview and making the introduction

After locating the correct respondent, the next phase in the interviewing process is for the interviewer to obtain the cooperation of the respondent. This involves the following:

1. introducing the concept of and sponsor for the study
2. introducing the focus of the study

3. explaining the basis for selection, and the need for the prospective respondent's participation

4. advising of confidentiality

5. requesting and obtaining participation from the respondent

The overall process requires skill, especially in those situations in which the individual is not particularly interested in participating. In such cases, the interviewer has to utilize a number of approaches designed to obtain the confidence of the respondent – *while ensuring that the information given in doing so is no more or no less than that for other respondents*, that is, to achieve and maintain consistency and the standardized interview.

Personal and interpersonal characteristics have been found to be important in this introductory phase. However, once the interview has started, the techniques used to interact with the respondent have to be changed to those consistent with the standardization of the survey.

Administering the Interview

Focusing on the content of the interview situation, Fowler and Mangione [1990] identify the main sources of error for interviewers as:
- not reading questions as worded
- probing directively
- biasing answers by the way they relate to respondents
- recording answers inaccurately

Each of these aspects will be reviewed briefly below.

Question wording

The efforts put into question wording for the design of a good instrument should be fully realized by the interviewer. The onus is therefore on him or her to ensure accurate representation of these questions. This includes:
- not changing the wording of questions
- not changing the tone of the questions (e.g. adding emphases)
- not adding questions
- not leaving out questions
- not changing the sequence in which questions are asked

If the concept of 'how to ask the question' is extended to the questionnaire in general, then other factors also become applicable, including:

Using the response category 'other'. Many questions might include an option for 'other'. This may be necessary if it is felt that the response options listed in the closed question are not exhaustive (and they very rarely are). This 'other' option is really an open sub-question (within the closed one) attempting to capture, in the final analysis, all the response possibilities. Interviewers very often neglect to seek the answer to this 'other' option – they simply do not ask the question! It is necessary to try and convey the importance of these responses to the interviewers during the training session.

How to deal with the response category 'don't know'. Another similar type of problem is often encountered with the response category 'don't know', but here the situation is far more complex. It is the researcher's responsibility to instruct the interviewers about wording the question in situations where there is a 'don't know' option.

Interviewers have to know whether or not to advise the respondent that this category exists. Research has indicated [Schumann and Presser 1981] that such instructions make a tremendous difference to the respondents' utilization of the option. The practical approach to the problem would be to use the content of the question, as well as the answers to the following questions, as guides regarding the instructions:

● Do the respondents *need* to know that they can say 'I don't know'?
● Will the respondents use the 'don't know' option as an easy way out of answering the question?
● Will the respondents feel forced to provide an answer even if they have no opinion on the topic in question?
● Will the interviewers use the 'don't know' as the easy way out if the respondent seems uncertain of the answer to the question?

Whatever the decision for the respective questions in the instrument, the interviewers *have to administer the questions consistently,* which means such instructions should be provided during training, and should also be written either in the questionnaire itself or in an accompanying 'manual' or 'guide to interviewing'.

The interviewing instructions. The guidelines for interviewing should be very clearly recorded in at least one of two places: on the questionnaire or in an interviewing guide designed specifically for the survey.

It is often best to include these on the questionnaire itself, but there are a few disadvantages to this practice. The main disadvantage of inclusion on the questionnaire is that the length (and apparent burden) of the instrument is increased. Another disadvantage is the chance of the instructions being read aloud by the interviewer!

Habituation. When there are a number of questions with the same or similar format, there is an increased likelihood of habituation taking place, of the interviewer and/or respondent becoming used to the situation. An example of a probable source of such an error follows:

There are ten consecutive questions asking the respondent to indicate whether he or she agrees or disagrees with the statements read by the interviewer. The acceptable responses are 'strongly agree', 'agree', 'disagree', 'strongly disagree' and 'don't know'. After responding appropriately to six of these statements, the respondent says 'I definitely agree'. Luckily, there is an emphasis placed on the 'definitely', which allows the alert interviewer to probe, finding that the respondent really means 'strongly agree' and not just 'agree'. In response to the interviewer's queries the respondent asks the following question: "I have to say the same word every time . . . over and over again?" Habituation has occurred here, with the respondent becoming somewhat tired of the repetitiveness of the question sequence, thereby resulting in attempts to depart from the structure. This type of situation can also lead to interviewers changing the question wording, skipping questions and assuming responses – all of which could introduce error.

The logic of the questionnaire. There must be some logic to the questionnaire; if this logic is absent from the interview, there could be mistakes in the answers, misinterpretations, and so on. For example, if a respondent is asked to account for all daily activities in number of hours per day, the total number of hours must sum to 24. Such situations would likely require probing for more detailed answers.

Probing

Any expansion of the written question by the interviewer to facilitate comprehension and/or response by the respondent within the context of interviewing can be called 'probing' (Box 7.1). This action can take the form of:

- additional questions
- explanations of words or phrases not stated clearly in the questionnaire
- comments intended to clarify the question as asked, or the situation as being investigated
- examples of similarities and situations intended to assist the respondent in answering the question

The important point to remember about probing is that there is *good* probing and there is *bad* probing. The former types of probing are known as 'non-directive' while the latter are 'directive'. The respondent must *not be led* to any specific answer by the probe being used for the question, but *rather must be assisted in understanding the intent of the question.*

The Caribbean situation in which respondents may not be literate increases the need for extreme vigilance regarding non-verbal cues from the respondents.

Probing is a very difficult technique to learn and to apply effectively and consistently. It would basically be impossible for all interviewers, on any single study, to apply the *same probes* for the *same questions* in the *same way*. Hence, the *concept* of probing is what needs to be clearly understood and conveyed to the team of interviewers.

Box 7:1 **Probing**	Examples of probes for interviewing . . . Tell me more about that . . . . . . Any other reason? . . . Why is that? . . . Yes? . . . And? . . . So . . . what would your answer to the question be? . . . You said that . . . can you tell me more? . . . Which ONE of those two answers would be closer to how you feel? . . . I'm not sure I understand . . .

Relating to respondents

The interaction between the interviewer and the respondent is not often highlighted, but is of critical importance to the process of data collection. There is in fact, a *relationship* which is built over the duration of the interaction, during which the interviewer needs to:

1. create and maintain an environment of trust with the respondent

2. convince the respondent of the benefits of participating in the survey, likely without obvious reward

3. encourage the confidences of the respondent

4. convince the respondent of the need to provide complete and accurate information relating to the topic area

5. engage the respondent in an intricate question and answer session during which new and/or unusual modes of responding are being encouraged

6. monitor closely the responses being provided, and be alert to possible inconsistencies and/or inaccuracies in responses

Within the context of building and nurturing this relationship, even the most seasoned interviewer is apt to encounter situations in which the lines between objective and subjective interviewing become somewhat blurred. There are a number of situations in which special care has to be given to the administration process, and some examples are identified below:

- Interviewing period: It is best to give the respondent a *good and realistic* idea of the amount of time required for the interview before commencing. For very long interviews, there will be a temptation to ascribe a shorter time period than the interview is known to last – just to get cooperation. This approach could result in worse consequences later in the interview, for example, the respondent might withdraw cooperation during the interview, or might provide inaccurate answers just to hasten the process and take it quickly to its conclusion.

- Socially desirable responses: There are some situations in which respondents might be ashamed of providing accurate responses, having perceived social dissonance between himself or herself and the interviewers and/or having developed a relationship with the latter that could be jeopardized with the correct information. This could result in the respondent providing answers which he or she believes the interviewer would find satisfying within the social context – inaccurate information. For example, if the respondent has answered to questions about television shows, a subsequent question about possession of a TV set might elicit an answer such as "We have one here, but it gone to fix." This response might mean exactly what it states, but it could also mean, for example, that the respondent is embarrassed to admit that the household watches TV programmes on a neighbour's set.

Another interesting source of error can be found where interviewers assume or presume the answer to a question without actually asking the question or by answering at the same time as asking.

Such a situation is more likely to occur if the interviewer thinks that the *respondent may be wary of answering* – for example,

- 'You have a toilet here, don't you?'

- 'Your age . . . you are about 30 . . . aren't you?'

- 'I assume that everybody in your household washes their hands before eating?'

These examples highlight a number of interviewing problems, and not only those due to social perceptions:

1. the interviewer is using his or her own standards in judgment
2. the respondents are the ones who should be answering the questions
3. the interviewer is actually apologizing for having to ask some of the questions (see below)
4. the interviewer is forcing the respondent, and making it very difficult, too, to contradict what have now become statements instead of questions

Apologizing for questions: If the humanness of the interviewer is considered, there could be some surveys in which he or she would rather not participate. The same could be applied to actual questions within an interview situation. If the latter were encountered, there might be a temptation to apologize for the questions and/or having to ask them. This could result in bias, and distance the respondent from the interview situation, making him or her less interested in the survey and/or continued participation.

External discussions: The same example provided above is one of many which could also lead to external discussions between the respondent and interviewer, outside of the focus of the interview. This is not a situation which should be encouraged, as it may lead to bias – especially if the subject is topical or contradictory to any of the issues being assessed in the survey.

Environmental concerns: The ideal context for interviewing is within a private environment. This is not always possible, especially in areas with high population density such as low income housing areas in the Caribbean. Given the close proximity of other persons, there will be a tendency for the respondent to approve their presence within the interview. Whatever the reasons given to the interviewer, this situation should be discouraged in order to preserve the confidentiality of the interview. In addition, there is the likelihood that some of the answers will be inaccurate, biased or incomplete. The onus and added burden would then be on the interviewer to recognize such inconsistencies and move to correct them – thereby extending the duration of the interview, and threatening the integrity of the interview. The situation with privacy and confidentiality is especially acute where the interview contains sensitive items and/or where a spouse or other family member(s) may not already have been privileged to the information being provided by the respondent. Extraneous noises such as loud music or shouting should also be avoided in conducting the interview. It may be difficult to avoid some of these situations depending on the actual location, but relocating to a quieter environment is advisable, or postponing the interview – since such a problem would result in the interviewer having to shout, or the respondent being unable to hear the questions, and these could lead to errors.

Also to be considered is the fact that the interviewing assignment will not always be a comfortable one. The interviewer may be forced to stand, or to sit on a stone or on the doorstep in order to facilitate the process and conduct the interview.

Recording answers

The process of recording answers on a questionnaire is usually regarded as being so mundane that it is rarely highlighted. Yet, like other aspects of data collection, it is a primary source of errors. This topic comprises a number of issues, including:

- *where* to record the answers
- *how* to record the answers
- *when* to record the answers
- *missing data*

These are addressed in more detail below.

Where to record answers

The layout within the questionnaire design should facilitate the process of recording as much as possible. Therefore, the spaces allotted to recording should be clearly identified, with sufficient space not only to write in the number or words to be recorded, but also to allow easy reading for data entry. The types of layout which are used for recording answers include:

- open spaces
- ruled spaces (i.e. with broken or unbroken lines on which to write)
- boxes (either completely or partially closed)
- use of precoded symbols such as numbers

The choice as to which ones are used is design driven as well as related to the type of question being asked, and may vary even within the same questionnaire. Interviewers should be made aware of which spaces or boxes are to be used for recording the answers for each question.

How to record answers

In addition to knowing where to record the responses from the respondents, interviewers also need to be informed of 'how' to record the answers:

- whether to use a pen or a pencil
- whether erasing or crossing out answers are acceptable practices
- whether to write the answer in a space or in a box
- whether to tick, place an 'X', or shade boxes
- whether to tick or circle a number
- whether there is a separate space for coding data, and whether or not these sections should be used by them

When to record answers

The only adequate option here is to record answers immediately and during the interview. There is a very strong tendency for interviewers to wait until after completing a set of interviews to record the answers to certain questions, and 'clean' their questionnaires. This is a very dangerous and costly practice for many reasons, including the following:

- It tests the limits of human memory.

- Despite their best efforts, interviewers who are conducting a series of interviews, will not be able to accurately filter out the relevant responses from the respective respondents to record answers on the questionnaire – after the fact.
- It usually results in either missing data or inaccurate data.
- The most accurate way of addressing such errors as would result from this practice would be a call back for the correct information. This option is costly, time consuming, inefficient, and reduces the credibility of the researcher or the organization. Furthermore, the problem is likely to be identified only with very tight supervision, and because this is so seldom effected, the real outcome is incomplete or inaccurate data.

Missing data

One of the most devastating practices in the conduct of surveys is related to missing data. It is a challenge to explain how difficult it is to treat such omissions. There are two types of missing data:

1. those that are not forthcoming since the respondent does not know the answer or does not wish to disclose information

2. those that are due to the failure of the interviewer to record completely or accurately

Since the latter is an avoidable error, it will be reviewed here. The problem is best understood with an example, as shown in Box 7.2. The three questionnaires used in this example all have missing data. In analysing the situation, some of the problems appear to be due to questionnaire design, given the consistency of some of the errors. This also indicates deficiencies with interviewing which result in problems at the data analysis stage.

BOX 7.2
Problems identified
due to missing data

SITUATION:

A set of interviews has been conducted, and the missing responses for questions 2, 3, 5, 7, 12, 19 and 25, as shown from different questionnaires, IDs 1–3, are shown below. The impact on data analysis is important to consider.

ID	SAMPLE QUESTIONS FROM QUESTIONNARE						
	2	3	5	7	12	19	25
1	X	X	X		X	X	X
2			X				X
3			X		X		X

X: missing data

ANALYSIS:

1. Q.5 and Q.25 are creating problems, and should be corrected/eliminated during the pretest.

2. The errors for Q.25 maybe an indication that the Q. is too long.

Introduction to Social Research

3. The interviewer responsible for the questionnaire with ID #1 should not be used in the assignment;

4. If cross-tabulatons were being conducted with Q.3 and Q.12 there would only be (1) usable questionnaire (i.e. ID #2) from this set – because of missing data.

The problems with non-response

There are many types of non-response in surveys. The most common are refusals, and inability to locate the required respondent. The interviewer's task extends to reducing the incidence of both by the following means:

- convincing the respondent of the need for interview
- convincing the respondent of the uniqueness of their response, but only with respect to the sampling – and not extending to data analyses
- negotiating a more convenient time for interview
- conducting call backs
- appropriately tailoring the interview if required
- encouraging continued cooperation of the respondent if there is danger of the respondent discontinuing the interview

Most interviewers and surveys will have problems with refusals as well as other types of non-response. The issue of migration is particularly important in the Caribbean. It is necessary for the researcher to provide the interviewer with stated procedures for the following:

empty house or vacant lot

household removed or migrated

household occupied at difficult hours only (e.g. very late at night)

excessive requests for call backs

outright refusals

refusals to continue interview

suspected inaccuracies and untruths during the interview (especially following refusals)

correct household member away from immediate location or country for extended period

Again, the decisions related to such outcomes need to be standardized, so that all interviewers approach the problems in the same way.

A number of these and other errors are encountered during interviewing sessions in the Caribbean. The situation often exists despite the researcher's best intent, commitment to accuracy and to training. There needs to be concern, for example, about the following interviewer practices:

a. not reading introductions/instructions as indicated – the tendency being to abbreviate, to choose one's own words and/or those more comfortable for each interview, with little regard for consistency of the information being divulged to the respondent

b. changing words, phrases or entire questions to patois or Creole presuming that this will facilitate respondents' apparent comprehension of the question

c. assuming that the answer to the question is known by the interviewer and failing to ask the question as indicated – a decision likely to be based on previous responses by the same or different respondents

d. changing the sequence in which questions are asked, and doing so in an ad hoc manner, based on the respondents' failure to respond, or to do so immediately

e. failure to use probing non-directively and consistently, the preference being to use the most convenient method for the situation

f. failure to record responses immediately and completely, the preference often being to complete the interview in the shortest time possible, with recording of data being done outside of, and after the interview situation (when responses not recalled accurately are likely to be concocted)

A number of options are available to the researcher in addressing such errors, including:

a. appropriate training, with actual question and answer sessions, simulating the interview

b. being as careful with the training of seasoned interviewers as with 'new' trainees

c. attending to details in the construction of questionnaires, for example wording introductions which are 'comfortable' for the interviewer

Aspects of Data Management

The data management procedures will not be dealt with in detail here. The coding procedure is more important. This has implications for questionnaire design, as well as for the interviewing phase.

Coding frames need to be designed concurrently with the design of the questionnaire. Decisions regarding pre-coding, as well as the format for recording responses, need to be incorporated into the design of the questions, and these must be conveyed clearly.

Coding

The process of coding entails assignment of numeric (occasionally alphanumeric) symbols to the responses obtained from the questions. This is sometimes done at the design stage, in which case it is called 'pre-coding'.

Pre-coding

The practice of pre-coding questions is appropriate for closed questions, for example:

'How often do you see your Member of Parliament (MP)?'

Once per week	1
Once per month	2
Once every three months	3
Less often than above	4

In such situations, the interviewer must circle (or tick) the appropriate number corresponding to the respondent's answer. This approach makes it unnecessary for a coder or editing clerk to convert the response into a code, as it would have already been done.

Coding open-ended questions

Open-ended questions require that more detailed coding procedures be followed. The researcher and coder, respectively, have to decide on and assign a series of numbers corresponding to the responses obtained. This is best started during the pretest phase, during which the range of options likely to be found will emerge. It will be necessary for these codes to be unique identifiers for the respective responses. One note to remember is that the *number of digits should be consistent throughout*. If there are more than 9 response categories, but less than 99, then the codes for the single digit responses need to have '0' added at the beginning, for example, 01, 02, 03 . . . 08, 09, 10 . . . 14.

The entire coding process is excessively tedious for:
- large surveys
- situations with many response alternatives
- complicated questions
- a large group of coders working simultaneously

These codes have to be written (or preferably typed) and circulated during the process so that all members of the coding team will have access to the codes as soon as they are added. The complete listings also have to be available for use at the data analysis stage.

Other data management notes

During this relatively tedious process, there is a tendency for researchers to reduce the amount of input and interest taken in the overall process, looking forward instead to the data analysis and reporting phases. This is a mistake. The researcher has to be at least assured that the person responsible for the process shows keen attention to details, otherwise the age-old saying 'garbage in garbage out' (GIGO) will become a reality in the most obvious phase to which it applies.

The related processes include:
- collating the questionnaires, preferably into batches
- editing the questionnaires, with much attention to missing data, the logic of the questionnaires and the responses, legibility, and appropriate recording
- preparing and/or reviewing the coding frame
- preparing the computer programme for, and entering the data
- preparing the computer programme and analysing the data
- 'eye-balling' the entered data, and running appropriate computer analyses to determine the 'cleanliness' of the data

📖 Data collection in surveys is comprised of several complex and detailed interactions between researcher and interviewer, and actually begins with the design of the questionnaire, and further includes interviewer training, identification of respondents, gaining their cooperation, conducting and recording the interview.

📖 The main methods for collecting survey data are face-to-face, telephone, and mail. Although the latter two are often used in developed countries, there is still great reliance on face-to-face interviewing in the Caribbean. This is due to limitations, including access to telephones and low literacy.

📖 There are many personal and interpersonal characteristics which make a good interviewer, and allow an interviewer to conduct a good interview, and these include personality, appearance, speech and mannerisms, discretion, and legible handwriting.

📖 The requirements for conducting a good interview include attention to question wording, appropriate use of response categories such as 'other' and 'don't know', providing adequate instructions, and appreciating the 'logic' of the questionnaire and responses. The technique of 'probing' must also be used appropriately to ensure complete and accurate responses. Recording responses accurately and in a timely manner is also necessary to reduce the errors obtained in the process.

📖 Data management is the phase which involves collation, editing, coding and data entry, and these all require careful attention to details.

📖 Budgetary and time constraints too often limit the rigour that must be applied to survey interviewing, especially in the developing countries in the Caribbean and elsewhere. Careful interviewer training and field supervision can help to decrease tendencies towards relaxed application of the survey method.

Exercise

Working in pairs, identify a good questionnaire of approximately three to four pages in length previously used for another study. Twelve copies of this instrument will be needed. Conduct a total of 6 interviews, i.e. 3 interviews each, with a sample of respondents relevant to the study for which the questionnaire was intended. Within the pair, the roles of interviewer and observer will be rotated for alternate interviews.

For each interview, the observer will be responsible for making as many notes as necessary on a blank questionnaire to provide feedback to the interviewer on: gaining cooperation, introducing the study, asking each question (including wording, phrasing, sequence), probing, non-verbal communication, and the interview environment. The observer must also record answers provided by the respondent. After *each* interview, the interviewer and observer discuss the session, comparing notes, procedures used, and results obtained.

Chapter Eight

Elements in Designing a Questionnaire

In social research, we frequently tend to use a questionnaire as the instrument for data collection. For the survey, the questionnaire is critical. Even for qualitative studies it might be used in addition to other methods. Let us think back to Figure 1.1 (see page 5). Questionnaire design only occurs after the conceptualization stage has been satisfactorily completed. This would mean that the variables in the hypothesis have been operationalized and their attributes identified. For example, suppose the hypothesis is: "Sustained school attendance in students from families below the poverty line is directly related to the type of school feeding programme in that school." Taking only one variable from this hypothesis as an example, type of school feeding programme is operationally defined to mean programme instituted in school which provides balanced lunches and breakfasts to students at no cost. To design the questionnaire the researcher would need to go further and clarify the attributes of the dependent and independent variables as well as any additional variables which will influence the types of questions that are going to be asked, for example, content of meals, time served, size of programme, availability and attractiveness.

Obviously there must be some limit to the number of questions that you would like to include. This is directly dependent on how well you have operationalized your variables and defined a specific hypothesis. You cannot measure everything in one questionnaire. You must be clear and precise in determining what you intend to measure.

Designing a questionnaire requires both technical and artistic skills. Some of the words used to describe the process and even the questionnaire itself, for example, 'formulate', 'construct', 'design', 'instrument' and 'tool', attest to this. There are five essential elements of questionnaire design which are easy to remember by an 'A B C D E' formation:

1. *Answers* – the aim in interviewing is to obtain answers to all questions applicable to the respondent. The implications for questionnaire design include wording, sequence, the use of categories, and recording issues.

2. *Basics* – any questionnaire can be made more friendly, thereby encouraging ease in interviewing, responding and recording.

3. *Content* – this represents the *focus* of the questionnaire, and has to be determined and refined prior to commencing design. It is particularly easy to lose the perspective of design if the content has not been refined.

4. *Design* – this could well be said to be the forgotten element of questionnaire construction. It relates essentially to aesthetics such as layout, style, length and burden.

5. *Exploration* – this relates to the more onerous and sometimes sophisticated issues involved in achieving the objectives through instrument design. Included here are issues such as measuring attitudes; pretesting questions/questionnaire/the interviewing process; and culture components.

Rules of Questionnaire Design

It is important to remember the following points throughout the process of questionnaire design:

1. The researcher has to remain objective throughout the design process.

2. The instrument will be used by *different interviewers* so it must be clear and easy to follow.

3. The questions will be answered by *different respondents*.

4. Respondents are chosen as being representative of some population, therefore standardization is essential to the overall process.

5. The standardization process is made much easier with a *simple* instrument which interviewers as well as respondents can relate to and utilize with ease.

6. A tremendous amount of work is put into the conduct of a good survey, and the questionnaire is a critical element in the process; it is better therefore to design a good questionnare at the start, rather than have regrets without choices at the end.

These are the basic rules of good questionnaire design:

1. Every question must ask one and only one question. It is very easy to confuse the respondent, asking more than one question in an apparently simple sentence. For example, Which method of transportation would you prefer in the evenings or mornings? Bus and train? You have two questions which are related to each other. They deserve to be separated into two independent questions, that is, method of transportation preferred in two different time segments.

2. Questions must use a language that is simple and appropriate. Since the purpose of scientific research is to elicit valid and reliable information, it makes little sense using words, slang, or terms that the respondent will not understand. Use of jargon, for example, needs to be restricted to those situations where it is necessary, and where it will be understood. The researcher needs to ensure that the language of the questionnaire takes into account the type of respondents, and is therefore clearly understood. Let us look at the Caribbean, for example, and the extent to which language differs in this region. Many territories are multilingual with at least one creole language, in addition to English or Spanish, French or Dutch. The language we use in the questionnaire therefore becomes very important. If the researcher is not a native to the country, it is wise to have such a person assist with questionnaire construction.

3. Questions must be concise, focused and *unambiguous*. It should be immediately clear what the question is asking. Sometimes we use words that are not clear in meaning. Take this question, for example: Does your daughter usually stay at home with you? What does 'stay at home' mean? Is the question asking whether or not she lives there with you; whether or not she stays inside; or is the question getting at where she lives?

4. Questions should never put words in the respondent's mouth. In other words, there should be no leading questions: 'The last time you smoked was last week, wasn't it?' Not only are you telling the person what you are hoping to hear but you are assuming that the person smoked last week. Instead, it is necessary first to ascertain whether or not the person smoked, and then if relevant, question the frequency with which the individual did so.

5. The questionnaire must not be too long, or otherwise burdensome to either the interviewer or interviewee. It should not tire, bore or irritate. There is no rule as to the number of questions you can use. For the questionnaire to be, and remain, interesting it should flow logically, building on successive questions, with a beginning, middle and end. In addition, it should not simply come to an end, but be clearly terminated with a 'Thank you'.

6. In designing a questionnaire it is best to try to get information at the most basic level. For example, one should try not to have too many

coded responses for numerical data. This aspect will be further discussed during this chapter.

Formatting

A questionnaire needs to be attractive. This attention to format and layout ensures greater clarity in comprehension, interviewing and in responding. The importance might be even greater when questionnaires are being mailed out. For example, sending an instrument with small print, cluttered layout, and/or poor directions would probably decrease the response rate, and the would-be respondent might throw it into the waste basket.

Formatting applies to

- layout
- typing (fonts should be uniform)
- use of headings to separate sections
- numbering of questions so that sequence is ensured
- placement of instructions

Instructions such as *skip questions and repeats* should be kept to a minimum.
Does your father raise livestock? (Tick one only)

☐ Yes full/time
☐ Yes part/time
☐ No

If *No* skip the following section. If *Yes* continue.
This could also be written:
If *No* go to section C. If *Yes* continue.

These kinds of instructions can become quite tedious. In designing a questionnaire, therefore, it is best to have entire sections which relate to subgroups, thus keeping relevant questions together.

All of these guidelines for questionnaire design take practice to master, and this is where the art of questionnaire design comes into play. It is always helpful to review questionnaires that have already been prepared.

Increasingly nowadays, we design questionnaires for large samples with the intent that the responses will be entered into one's choice of data management software. This has implications for formatting, as eventually in the editing-coding stage all those ticks, Xs, and so on must be transformed to numbers. Allowance should therefore be made in the initial design phase for appropriate recording on the questionnaire.

The length of and spacing between lines is also important. A respondent may be asked to fill in a response, for example to the question: What is your address?

It would be important to leave enough space to write in a full standard address in a normal writing fashion.

Good questionnaires must, as a rule, be accompanied by a) an introduction; and b) a covering letter.

The introduction

This serves to introduce the interviewer and the research. It establishes the interviewer's name, the agency/institution with which he or she is associated, and explains concisely the purpose of the research. It also tells the respondent what method was used for selection to the sample, explains what will be done with the findings from the research, and assures confidentiality. It does *not*, however, make any promises which cannot be fulfilled and is careful not to lie about research intent.

The introduction is not long: it is either a long paragraph or a page, and is usually placed at the beginning of the questionnaire.

The covering letter

A covering letter is often used for institutional surveys, and is sent, for example, to the agency or institution from which the sample is to be selected. It encloses the proper title for the research and says who is responsible for the study. It explains the reason for the study and establishes the procedure which will be used for sample selection. Importantly, it requests permission for the study to take place within that agency/organization/institution. It also identifies the actual interviewers.

**BOX 8:1
Basics and layout of a
typical questionnaire**

Title _____

ID: _____

INT. #: _____

SECTION I. *Introduction*

Hello, my name is _____ , and I'm from _____. We are conducting a survey about _____ , and you/your household have/has been chosen according to _____.

SECTION II. *Demographic information on respondent*

This section can be placed either at the beginning or at the end. It would include some questions which would relate to position in household, age, gender, head of household, last born in household and so on, and any other questions that may be useful in placing later responses in context.

SECTION III. *Icebreaker questions*

This section would include more general questions which are relevant to the focus of the study, but which would not be threatening to the respondent. Questions could be drawn from the substantive or demographic areas, for example, and would serve to put the respondent at ease. Such questions should be relatively few in number, otherwise the respondent might begin to question relevance.

SECTION IV. *Substantive questions*

The more serious issues to be investigated would be positioned at this point. There is no real limit to the *number* of questions, but the following are important:

1. Structure the questions in a logical sequence, trying to move from the general to the specific.

Box 8.1 cont'd

2. Remember to focus on what is *important* rather than on what is interesting.

SECTION V. *Demographic questions*

The questions which relate to demographic background are very important to the context and analyses of the survey questionnaire. However, the relevance of such questions may not always be evident to the respondent. Thus, it is important to introduce this section by indicating that the upcoming questions will help the researcher to place into context the previous answers, for purposes of the analysis.

Some standard, written closure should be provided so that all respondents are universally acknowledged. For example:

"We have now come to the end of the interview, and want to thank you for your cooperation. Are there any questions which you want to ask?"

The Questions and Their Responses

There are a range of ways that question responses can be formatted. Basically there are two main types of questions used in surveys: 'open' (or open-ended), and 'closed'(or close-ended). In the open-ended question, the respondent is asked to answer a question that places no boundaries on the type or format of his or her response. In the closed question, however the researcher has created a specific format within which the respondent is allowed to provide an answer. In the close-ended response the interviewee is forced to respond in a particular manner.

In close-ended questions, the interviewer can accept only those answers which can be recorded using the categories provided. The ability of the researcher to 'close' or pre-code the question depends on his or her having sufficient information about the topic to feel confident that most of the likely responses will be included in the options provided, as well as on the nature of the replies required.

For example, if I simply ask: How satisfied are you with the school lunch? and leave it open I could get responses such as 'not so satisfied', 'depends on who is the chef that day', 'the government could do better', 'my mother says I must take it so I do', 'I like the breakfast most of the time' and so on.

Had I asked: How satisfied are you with the school lunch? and forced the respondent to reply in a fixed format, say:

satisfied all of the time	1
usually satisfied	2
not usually satisfied	3
not satisfied at all	4

there would have been less opportunity for the wide range experienced above.

Characterizing categories

The close-ended answer must, however, satisfy two basic characteristics of all categorization and this should be kept in mind when editing and coding the responses. Categories must be mutually exclusive and exhaustive.

Introduction to Social Research

Mutually exclusive

The categories that you have included ensure that a person's response can fall in one and only one category. If you say 'usually satisfied' this is quite different from 'not usually satisfied'.

Exhaustive

This characteristic ensures that any possible response has been accounted for.

Response categories

A similar type of approach needs to be taken in identifying response categories ideally needed for capturing answers. One restriction to defining these is the general lack of information on the real scope of responses from the respondents. While it might be quite easy to calibrate a response scale 'from the desk' without referring to pretests or some other form of investigation to justify the categories being chosen, this is not an adequate method to use.

There are many options available for response categories. In general, the categories can be labelled either verbally or numerically.

Types of response options

1. Open-ended

Why do you think it is so difficult to maintain a positive relationship with your spouse? _____

Record the response verbatim.

2. Fill-in or completion

This is similar to above, but it is more structured.

Previous job _____ Present job _____
Name of employer _____

3. Scaled response

This would measure the degree of importance, and the person is asked to circle the number which best represents how important X is to them.

very important 1—2—3—4—5 *not important at all*

4. Ranking

The task is to circle one of the following which best represents the respondent's feeling. Please note that: SA = strongly agree, A = agree, D = disagree

The person who commits murder should be hanged   SA   A   D

Or the task might be:

Rank each of the following statements from 1 to 3, 1 being the most important to you, and 3 being the least.

a. In an intimate relationship the woman should be outwardly affectionate.

b. In an intimate relationship the man should pay all the bills.

c. In an intimate relationship the man should be outwardly affectionate.

5. Checklist response

The kind of job that I would prefer would be (check one)
   A job that stretches my imagination / __ /
   A job that is close to home / __ /
   A job that is very prestigious / __ /

6. Categorical response

Are you a willing volunteer?   1. YES   2. NO

Training

If you are going to have help in conducting the interviews, you will need to schedule training sessions to explain in detail how to administer the questionnaire. During these sessions, basic interviewing techniques should be reviewed; specific details on administering the instrument introduced; and there should also be practice sessions incorporating all elements. The format of the practice sessions should include:

- the art of relationship formation – the establishment of a good relationship between the interviewer and the respondent is critical to the process of question administration
- the general art of questionnaire administration – remembering that what is clear to the interviewer might be confusing to the respondent
- interviewers administering a questionnaire during training to simulate the actual event in role play sessions – they will therefore have the opportunity to test how comfortable the instrument is, and whether there need to be revisions, or re-interpretation in the field

Pretesting

The 'pretesting', 'field testing' or 'piloting' phase is one during which the instrument is, in effect, checked for adequacy and accuracy. Ideally, the pretesting is done at the point when the questionnaire is almost ready, with content, wording, layout and other design features near completion. Pretesting allows the researcher to assess the validity and reliability of the instrument. Aspects which can benefit significantly from pretesting include:

- checks on flow, question wording, phrasing and sequence
- validation of rating scales
- comprehensiveness of pre-coded questions
- adequacy of skip/go to patterns
- checks on length of time and possible fatigue

Interviewers should be asked to record any observations on the instrument, so that problems with specific questions can be easily identified. It is also important that the researcher conduct debriefing sessions with the interviewers after the pretests, to discuss in detail, the administration of the interviews.

The questionnaire is the primary means of data collection in the quantitative method. The questionnaire provides the opportunity for collecting exactly the same type of information from all the elements in the sample in exactly the same format. This helps to ensure consistency in administration and interpretation. This means that the researcher is then able to code the responses numerically and generate quantifiable information with certainty.

For the social researcher there are different ways of eliciting primary information. Basically these are administered questionnaires (sometimes called response schedules), mailed questionnaires, interview schedules (sometimes called interviewer briefs), telephone interviews.

In questionnaire construction we must bear in mind the question of replicability/reliability, as in scientific research the intent is always to be able to repeat the process with a similar sample and gain similar results. The questionnaire must therefore be well constructed following the rules as outlined in this chapter.

Exercises

1) Design three different types of response options for the following question: On average, how many times per week do you eat the following foods for lunch at school: buns, patties, biscuits, cooked lunch, other?

2) Do you see anything wrong with the following question? If you do please explain and reformulate:
Can you think of any way in which eating food influences your attendance at school?

Chapter Nine

Unobtrusive Research

Not all scientific research brings the social investigator in contact with a live subject. In many cases researchers use the remains of human beings to make statements about them, or they may use the complete observer method so as not to affect the object being studied. This type of research is know as unobtrusive research. The *Oxford Reference Dictionary* [1989] defines unobtrusive as "not making oneself or itself noticed". In this chapter we will examine three types of unobtrusive research – trace measures, content analysis and personal documents.

Trace Measures

This type of research involves the examination of the wearing down or the addition of physical objects as a result of their use. There are two types of physical traces – accretions and erosions.

Accretions

Accretions refer to items left behind as a result of human activity. Such items may include cups and bottles from house parties and costumes from carnival celebrations. Sociologists in the United States have conducted studies of garbage to see/determine what types of food people eat which can in turn give an indication of their social class or ethnic background. Hughes [1958], in talking about an analysis of garbage by janitors, states:

> It is by the garbage that the janitor judges, and as it were gets power over tenants . . . Janitors know about hidden love affairs by bits of torn up letter paper; of impending financial disaster or of financial four-flushing by the presence of many unopened letters in the waste (p. 51).

Archaeologists and physical anthropologists have long used physical traces to determine the lifestyles of ancient or destroyed civilizations.

Erosions

Erosions refer to the wearing down of items such as shoe soles and walking paths on lawns. Rural sociologists in the United States studied migration patterns in the west by examining wagon trails. It is possible to study the movement patterns of people in places such as housing schemes or a university campus by examining walking paths.

Limitations of trace measures

1. This approach opens up the possibility of multiple interpretations of a phenomenon. As a result it is very difficult to make causal statements from trace measures. As a consequence it is used mainly in exploratory studies.

2. Some types of research using trace measures may be seen as an invasion of privacy. For instance, disturbing sacred areas of a group to study religious beliefs may be viewed as sacrilegious by some groups.

Content Analysis

Content analysis is a research technique particularly well suited to the study of communication. Social researchers use content analysis to study any recorded form of human communication for the purpose of testing hypotheses, describing or simply cataloguing the information collected. Content analysis can be used for the analysis of speeches, poetry, television programmes and laws. With content analysis we are concerned with who says what to whom, why, how and with what effect. After concentrating on what and how, we can make inferences to determine effect.

According to Bailey [1987: 300],

> the basic goal of content analysis is to take a verbal non-quantitative document and transform it into quantitative data. Content analysis is

equivalent in document study to survey research. It is conducive to the use of formal hypotheses, large scientifically drawn samples, and quantitative data that can be analysed with computers and modern statistical techniques.

Bailey [1987: 301] further lists seven purposes for content analysis, apart from testing hypotheses. These include:

1. describing trends in communication content
2. relating known characteristics of messages they produce
3. auditing communication content against standards
4. analysing techniques of persuasion
5. analysing style
6. relating known attributes of the audience to messages produced for them
7. describing patterns of communication

Some questions that can be examined by using this technique include: (a) Are women portrayed passively compared to men on television? (b) Are violent television shows associated with more male than female advertisements? (c) To what extent do local newspapers reflect conservative or liberal biases in news coverage?

| **Box 9:1 Content analysis of a political debate** | The following is an article which used content analysis to analyse a nationally televised political debate, between the People's National Party and the Jamaica Labour Party, held during the Jamaica General Elections of 1993. **"An Analysis of the National Political Debate"** (Ian Boxill, *The Daily Gleaner*, 3 March 1994) On March 16th, Jamaicans saw their first debate between Prime Minister P. J. Patterson and Opposition Leader Edward Seaga. Although in many ways the debate was disappointing, there was much to be satisfied about in that it represented a first for the country. So far most of the analyses of the debate that I have seen have tended to be very subjective and based on people's intuition. This article is an attempt to analyse the debate from a more scientific standpoint, by using the technique of content analysis. I was assisted in this analysis by two sociology graduate students at the UWI, Sandra Minott and Andrene Lattibeaudiere. In analysing the debate the focus was on candidates, presentation of self, type of responses to questions, content of the responses, and performance of panelists. |

Presentation of self

Here I am concerned with the relative use of assertive language. I found that Mr Seaga tended to use more assertive phrases and words than Mr Patterson. When Mr Patterson did use assertive language, invariably it took the form of a rebuttal to Mr Seaga. In addition, Mr Seaga's body language tended to convey a greater sense of confidence, although occasionally

Introduction to Social Research

bordering on contempt for the panelists. Mr Patterson, on the other hand, tended to be more nervous and seemed to pay a great deal of deference to Mr Seaga.

Table 9.1 Number of assertive phrases

Patterson	18
Seaga	24

Type and content of responses

An examination of type of responses to questions showed that Mr Patterson answered a greater percentage of questions directly than Mr Seaga. In general, however, both persons gave few indirect responses. On the other hand though, Mr Seaga tended to be more precise and specific than Mr Patterson in answering the questions.

Table 9.2 Percentage of questions answered directly/indirectly

	Direct responses	Indirect responses
Patterson	75	25
Seaga	60	40

Table 9.3 Percentage of questions answered in specific/vague language

	Specific	Vague
Patterson	68	32
Seaga	82	18

Mr Seaga was much more confrontational and negative in his responses than Mr Patterson. He tended to use words such as 'awful shortages', and 'social disaster' as opposed to a much more conciliatory approach by Mr Patterson, who used words and phrases such as 'bipartisanship, and 'working together'. However, Mr Patterson came across somewhat timid and overly accommodating.

Table 9.4 Number of confrontational phrases/words

Patterson	4
Seaga	17

Mr Patterson gave more rebuttals than Mr Seaga. In the majority of cases these rebuttals were in direct response to statements made by Mr Seaga.

Table 9.5 Number of rebuttals

Patterson	11
Seaga	7

With respect to policy emphases, both speakers placed an overwhelming emphasis on economic matters (this was partly due to the types of questions asked by the panelists).

**Box 9.1
cont'd**

Mr Patterson was, in general, more balanced in respect of emphases. He tended to pay greater attention to social sector than Mr Seaga.

Table 9.6 Percentage of time spent on various sectors

	Economic	Social	Other
Seaga	62	15	23
Patterson	51	28	21

Interestingly, there was very little difference between Mr Seaga and Mr Patterson with respect to their views on the role of the state and the market. In fact very few references were made to indicate the link between the state and the market. It is therefore clear there are very few ideological differences between the two candidates.

Table 9.7 Number of references to the role of the state and the free market

	State	Free Market
Patterson	3	2
Seaga	3	3

The panel

Generally speaking, the panel tended to ask questions dealing with economic and political issues. These were followed by questions having to do with personality/character issues.

Table 9.8 Percentage of each type of question asked

Economics	50
Politics	25
Character/personality	15
Social	5
Other	5

Interestingly there were only five follow-up questions by the panelists, with four of them coming from the moderator, Professor Aggrey Brown.

Overall assessment of performance

In general, Mr Seaga was very assertive (sometimes overly so), more indirect in responding to questions, but much more specific in language. He also tended to be more confrontational and proactive, and placed much greater emphasis on economic policies compared to social ones.

On the other hand Mr Patterson appeared to be less assertive than Mr Seaga, passive and somewhat reactive. However, although like Mr Seaga he tended to emphasize economic polices, his responses on policy issues tended to be more balanced, paying greater attention to the social sector than Mr Seaga.

One of the weakest aspects of the debate was the panel which tended to ask long, drawn out and sometimes ambiguous questions, with few follow-ups. As a result this allowed both Mr Seaga and Mr Patterson to make unchallenged statements. Perhaps a much better prepared panel would have made for a more interesting debate.

There are obviously very few policy differences between the two candidates. This suggests to me that come election day people will be voting, fundamentally, on the basis of personality.

Research design and sampling in content analysis

Content analysis utilizes many of the sampling techniques discussed in earlier sections of this book. Let us say that we wanted to do a descriptive study of the incidents of sexist language in selected sociological texts. Here is an example of how we can go about completing the study.

Topic: Sexist language in sociological texts at the UWI

Determine variable to be measured – Sexist language

Determine unit of analysis – Phrases considered to be sexist

Determine operational definition of sexist language – Any phrase that may be interpreted to be treating men and women differently, simply on the basis of their sex.

Determine different categories of indicators – Sexist language which emphasizes gender differences in relation to occupations, intellectual abilities, family life.

Determine sampling frame – All sociological texts used for teaching during 1996–1997 in the Department of Sociology, UWI, Mona.

Determine sample – A systematic random sample of pages in each book, using a sampling interval based on a 20 percent sample.

Code data – Code instances of sexist language using a nominal scale for different categories and an interval scale for number of times the language is used.

Analyse data – Use various descriptive statistics to describe the data/the number, variation/differences between categories. We can also use inferential statistics to test hypotheses.

Present data – Use frequency distributions and graphs to present the types and frequency of sexist language used. Use the appropriate statistics to assist in the clarification of the findings.

Strengths and weaknesses of content analysis

Strengths

1. Content analysis is an inexpensive way of doing research.

2. It is easy to replicate a study using content analysis.

3. You can focus on relatively long time periods with ease with content analysis. For instance, one can look at sexist language in sociology textbooks at the UWI over the past 30 years with great ease.

4. Because content analysis is an unobtrusive technique, the researcher does not impact on the subject being studied.

Weaknesses

1. Content analysis is restricted to recorded communications.

2. Studies using content analysis may encounter problems of validity. That is, the operational definitions of variables may not reflect the situation at the time of writing. For example, someone who would have been probably labelled as politically radical fifty years ago might by today's standard be considered politically conservative. Consequently, a content analysis of ideological labels might be misleading unless the researcher places his or her analysis in historical context. While this is not impossible to do, it is invariably difficult.

3. The population for analysis is often biased because items are selectively deposited and retained. Hence the surviving data do not necessarily represent a sample of the originally created data. For example, a content analysis of communication between masters and slaves between 1740 and 1780 in Jamaica would be biased in favour of those available records left for study. The problem here is that the records could be biased for two reasons: first, those documents left may only be a sample of what was originally produced in the period under study. Secondly, the recorded units of communication will most certainly be written from the perspective of the masters, since not many slaves could read and write at the time.

Personal Documents

In many ways, the study of personal documents is similar to participant observation. Personal documents have the advantage of providing the researcher with the "spontaneity of first-person accounts and a depth of intimacy and innermost (even subconscious) feeling not generally available in survey research or non-personal document study" [Bailey 1987: 296]. One example of a personal document is *Edna Manley: The Personal Diaries*, edited by Rachel Manley. This masterfully organized work comprises the personal diaries of Edna Manley, wife of former Premier of Jamaica, Norman Manley, between the years 1939 to 1986. The diaries are packed with information on such diverse issues as Edna and Michael's personal struggles with Jamaican and Caribbean politics.

Personal documents rarely allow for large sample sizes. The cases for study are often chosen subjectively by the researcher in response to his or her personal interests. According to Bailey [1987], the approach lends itself to qualitative rather than quantitative analysis. Any analysis of personal documents will generally consist of taxonomies, as in the analysis of data from observational field studies. After the taxonomy is discussed, particular examples of personal documents can be chosen to illustrate the different types contained in the taxonomy or to illustrate some theoretical point [Bailey 1987: 298].

Often the personal document researcher is more concerned with making generalizations and theoretical points about the topic by using excerpts from the documents.

📖 When the researcher does not disturb or influence the people being studied, this is known as unobtrusive research.

📖 The study of personal documents and trace measures, along with content analysis are three forms of unobtrusive research.

📖 The study of trace measures involves the examination of the wearing down of or the addition of physical objects as a result of their use.

📖 Content analysis is a technique used to study any recorded form of human communication for the purpose of classification, explanation or description.

📖 The study of personal documents entails the examination of personal writings such as diaries and letters, usually to arrive at general conclusions or make theoretical points.

Exercises

1. Some people have argued that part of the lure of contemporary Jamaican dancehall music is that the lyrics are more explicitly sexual than other types of music heard and played in the Caribbean. But is this a fact or is it simply fiction? Well, here is an opportunity for you to practise content analysis while at the same time testing a view that is often taken for granted. First, find and transcribe the most popular dancehall songs in your country for the past five years. Do the same for the most popular non-dancehall songs. Then conduct a content analysis of both categories of songs to see which group has more sexually explicit lyrics. Remember that you have to define and operationalize a numbers of concepts including 'sexually explicit lyrics' and 'popular songs'. Here is a suggestion to get you started: you can define popularity in terms of the song that was ranked highest on the most prestigious local music charts or by the number of records, compact discs and/or cassette sales in the country. Good luck.

2. One of the things which fascinate social scientists is the path people take to get from one place to another. Apart from telling them about human interaction such information can help in the design of emergency rescue systems, particularly in large organizations. By looking at erosion left from footpaths, researchers can determine patterns of movement and in some cases the nature of human interaction. Here is a simple way of assessing human movement and interaction by using trace measures. Examine and record the walking paths of people on your campus. What do they tell us about movements of people? Here are two suggestions which will help you to answer this question: first, see if you can locate where these paths begin and where they end; secondly, examine the width of these paths and their distance from roads and buildings, recreation fields, bus stops, car parks and other potential destinations.

Chapter Ten

Analysing Data and Presenting Findings

In this chapter we focus on how to analyse data once we have collected them. Keep in mind the topic, the assumptions (if stated), the hypothesis (as operationalized) and the sample with which you worked. Analysis means summarizing observations, testing hypotheses, computing statistics and reaching conclusions. In previous chapters we discussed the editing and coding of data – steps critical to proper data analysis. We will now focus on three stages of data analysis:

1. Graphic presentation of data

2. Descriptive statistics

3. Inferential statistics

Preliminary steps

Having cleaned and edited the data, we will have to be sure that all open-ended questions are properly coded as it is not possible to transfer each and every response exactly as it is. Having done that, it is possible to run aggregates or summary tables on each variable or question. In survey designs we often run 'marginals' or frequency distributions on univariate data. Frequency distribution tables represent scores and their distributions in table form (see Table 10.1).

Tabular Presentation of Data

This is a frequency distribution on a single variable, *Score of Friendliness*. To construct the table, a tally count is needed. In this case 'friendliness' is measured in the form of an index and in the tables, it ranges between 20 and 50. A frequency distribution is the simplest table that we can construct.

Table 10.1 Frequency distribution on a single variable: Score of Friendliness

Categories/Scores	Tally Count	f
20	////	4
30	HHH HHH	10
40	///	3
50	HHH HHH HHH	15

Tally counting is used when counting in groups of five. Cumulative frequencies can also be devised from the same data. The cumulative frequency is the sum of the frequencies for a given category (see table 10.2).

Table 10.2 Cumulative Frequency distribution on a single variable: Score of Friendliness

Categories/Scores	Tally Count	f	cum. freq.
20	HHH	4	4
30	HHH HHH	10	14
40	///	3	17
50	HHH HHH HHH	15	32

Table 10.2 shows that 17 persons scored 40 or less while 32 persons scored 50 or less.

Graphic Presentation of Data

One alternative to presenting numerical data in tabular form is the graphic or picture form. To many people, graphs are less threatening and easier to understand than a set of numbers in a table. The most elementary of graphic presentations include pie charts, bar graphs, histograms, frequency polygons and line graphs.

Pie charts

A pie chart is a circular graph in which all of the slices or various sections add up to 100 percent. Pie charts are used in univariate analysis to illustrate differences or similarities between groups or categories. The illustration below is an example of a pie chart (see Figure 10.1a). In some computer programmes you can generate pies with the slice extracted or draw the pie in three dimension (see Figure 10.1b).

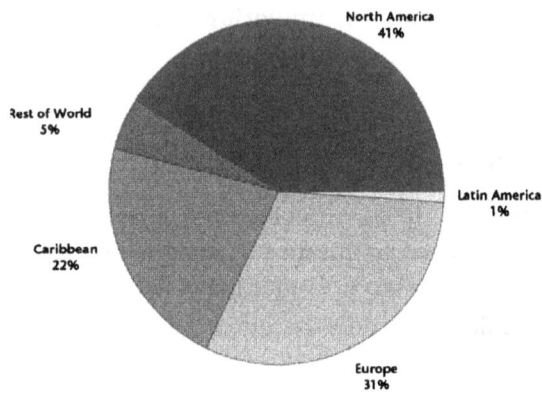

Figure10.1a

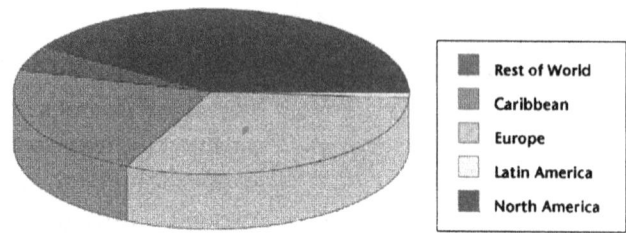

Figure10.1b

1994 St Lucia Tourist Arrivals: Based on Country of Origin

Bar graphs

Perhaps the most frequently used graphic presentations are bar graphs which can accommodate variables measured at any level. A bar graph or chart is most frequently used to represent nominally scaled independent variables. Bar graphs can be used to represent univariate, bivariate and multivariate data for analysis. The graphs below indicate the various ways in which bar graphs can be used, where Figure 10.2a shows a simple bar chart while Figure 10.2b is more complex, comparing two variables, namely, percentage unemployed in 1981 and 1991 across the age groups in the same chart. There are also horizontal bar charts and component or stacked bar charts which present more than one value on the same bar. Bars are always continuous but are drawn separate from each other, of the same thickness and at the same distance from each other.

Figure10.2a

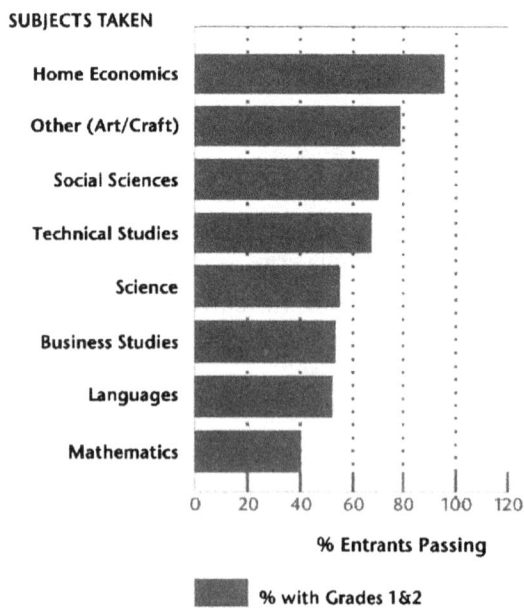

1994 CXC subject passes in St Lucia as percent of entries

Figure10.2b

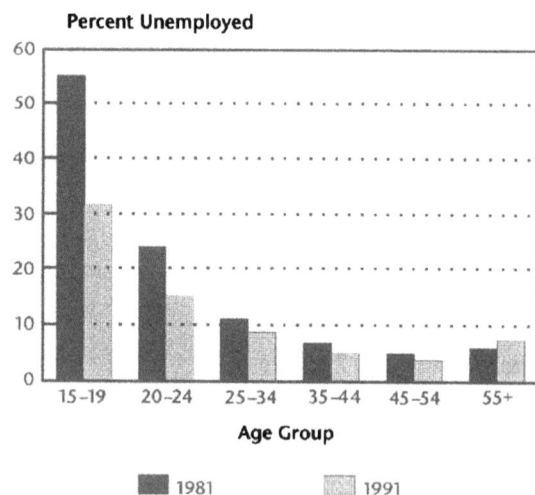

Dominican unemployment levels by age group, 1981-1991

Frequency polygons

When researchers are interested in showing continuity along a scale or the shape of a frequency distribution they use frequency polygons. Frequency polygons are usually associated with ordinal and interval data. To construct a frequency polygon first find the value of the independent variable on the X axis and from this point draw a line parallel to the Y axis. Then do the same for the dependent variable on the Y axis drawing a line from the point parallel to the X axis. These two lines should cross each other. Mark the point at which they intersect. Join all the points of intersection by a line. Figure 10.3 is an example of a frequency polygon.

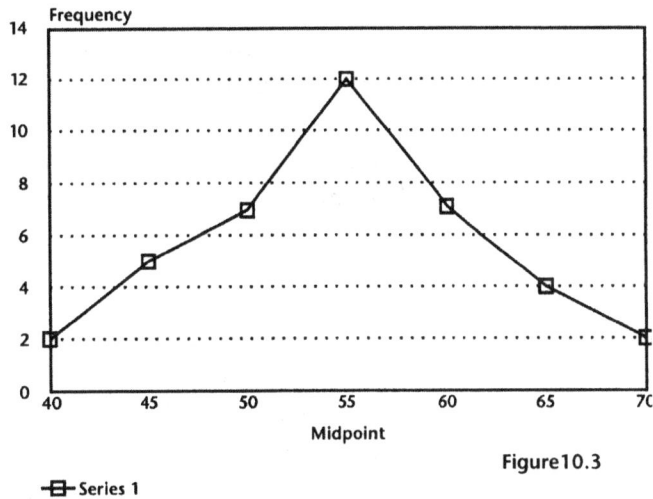

Figure 10.3

Students' examination scores: Frequency Polygon

Line graphs

Line graphs are used to display changes in a variable or variable between groups or over time [Fox and Levin 1994: 63]. As seen in Figure 10.4, social researchers use line graphs to display trends in data.

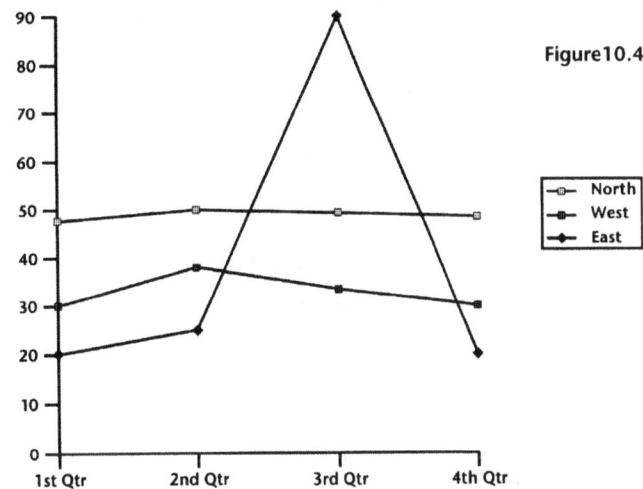

Figure 10.4

School attendance levels across quarters by area

Descriptive Statistics

Descriptive statistics are computations which help to organize and make our data understandable. They allow the researcher to describe characteristics of large samples and to make the data easy to interpret. The most frequently used descriptive statistics are measures of central tendency and measures of variability.

Measures of central tendency include the mode, median and mean which are all averages.

The mode

The mode is the most frequently occurring number in a distribution. It is the most easily computed (just look for the most frequent score) and it can be used with nominal, ordinal and interval level data. For instance, in Table 10.1 (p.119), the mode is 50 because there are fifteen students with that score. There are situations when a distribution can have more than one mode. For example, the modes for the following example are 5 and 18:

3, 4, 7, 5, 8, 5, 10, 18, 19, 17, 18, 16, 18, 5.

The median

The median is the midpoint of the distribution. It is the 50th percentile or the position at which half of the values lie above and half lie below. There is only one median in each distribution. It can be used with ordinal, interval or ratio level scores. Unlike the mode or mean, it is least affected by extreme scores. For this reason, the median is often used to arrive at an average in distributions which tend to be skewed. For instance, suppose we had the following distribution of examination scores, 12, 13, 14, 28, 45, 55, 56; the median, would be in the fourth position, which has a value of 28, since three scores lie above and three scores lie below it. An easy way of finding the middle score is to add the total number of scores, plus one and divide by two. In our example we would get 7+1/2 = 4.

Now suppose the distribution had an even number of scores such as 12, 13, 14, 28, 45, 46, 55, 56. The median would now fall between the 4th and 5th positions and have a score value of 28+45/2 or 36.5 which is halfway between these two values, even though no one actually got this score in the examination.

The mean

This is the most often used measure of central tendency and is also called the arithmetic average. To obtain the mean of a distribution, we add the scores reported and divide by the total number of scores (or N). The formula for the mean for raw data is therefore

Mean (which is written as $\bar{x}$) = $\Sigma X/N$

where

Σ (Sigma) is the Greek symbol for the command 'the sum of'

X is each score (value) in the distribution

N is the number of values in the distribution

Let us take a simple univariate distribution: 3, 7, 8, 8, 12, 15, 17. The mean would be 3+7+8+8+12+15+17 divided by 7 which is 10, the median would be 8 and the mode 8. If we changed the 17 to 26 and the 15 to 20, the median and the mode would remain the same, while the mean would now be 12. Thus the mean is most severely affected by extreme score values.

Given the data in Table 10.3, how would you compute the mean age of the children?

Table 10.3 Distribution of age of children

Age of child	f	fX
3	10	30
4	14	56
5	15	75
7	5	35
8	8	64
9	3	27
N=55		ΣfX=287

We need first of all to know the sum of the ages of the children. We cannot simply sum (f) as this would give us the total number of children rather than their ages. What we need to know is how many persons had a child in each age category and then sum that, that is (f) times each age (X), the same as (fX). This can then be divided by N. The formula becomes,

$\bar{x} = \Sigma fX$

in place of N

$\bar{x} = \Sigma X \ N$

Therefore $\bar{x} = \dfrac{287}{55}$

The mean age of the children is therefore 5.2 years.

To continue, think of a balance and a fulcrum.

```
#        #
### #####
     ▲
```

The fulcrum is the point at which all the weights balance out or, in this instance, the point at which all the scores balance out. Heavy scores, that is larger scores, are taller while lighter scores are shorter. The fulcrum can be likened to the mean, which is a measure of balance. Thus, if we add one more score on one side, the balance will tip and the fulcrum must be moved to accommodate it. If we add the same score on both sides, will we have to move the fulcrum? The answer is *no*. This means that when we have a distribution with a wide range of responses, the mean value must compensate for all of them, unlike the median. We should therefore be careful to decide which measure is chosen to represent central tendency (average) as each one does have a different meaning. The mean can only be used with interval or ratio-level data.

In computing the mean, if we have grouped the data, the same formula cannot be used as before because the data are now in categories.

Table 10.4 Computation of the mean from grouped data

Categories	X	midpoint	fX
5 to 10	5	7.5	37.5
11 to 16	18	13.5	243.0
17 to 22	3	19.5	58.5
23 to 28	11	25.5	280.5
29 to 38	22	31.5	693.0

$\Sigma fX = 1312.5$

The first change is that we need to find some measure which will best represent each category. Following the steps of Table 10.3, after having found the midpoint X, the formula for grouped data becomes

$\bar{x} = \Sigma\, fX/N$

$\bar{x} = 1312.5/59$

$\bar{x} = 22.25$

REMEMBER to be careful in your computations as carelessness might not be realized until too late. There is a great difference between 1.5 children, usually reported as two, and 1.05 usually reported as one.

The results for the mean can be very different from that of the mode and median. This is because the mean is affected by extreme scores in the distribution. The figures below are graphic representations of the relative positions of the mean, mode and median in different distributions of scores.

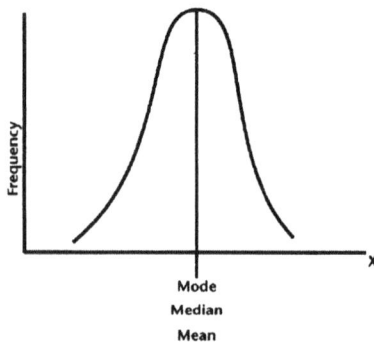

Figure 10.5a

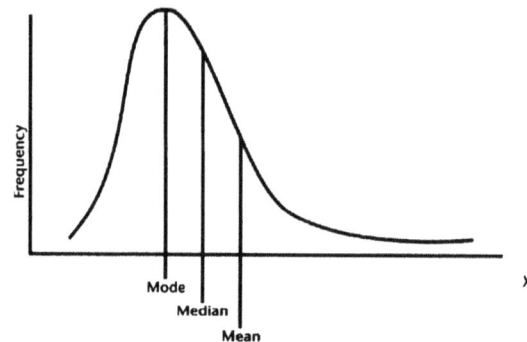

Figure 10.5b

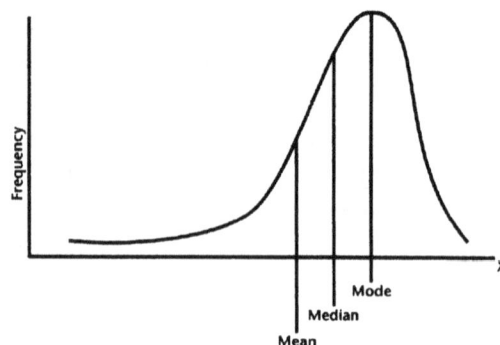

Figure 10.5c

Relative positions of the mean, mode, and median in distribution of scores

In Figure 10.5a we have a normal or bell-shaped curve in which the three measures of central tendency fall at the same point. Figures 10.5b and 10.5c introduce what is termed a skewed distribution where there are more of either higher or lower scores. The three measures are therefore at different positions.

The following points were developed by Sarantakos [1993: 355], using the works of such writers as Foddy [1988], Guilford [1965], Sofos [1990] and others, to be used as a guide when trying to decide which measure to use.

1   The mode is chosen if the variable is nominally scaled.

2   The mean or median is chosen if the variable is ordinal, interval or ratio.

3   If the distribution shows a central tendency, the mean or median is a better choice: if there is no central tendency, the mode should be employed.

4   If the distribution is skewed, the median is a better choice. This is particularly so for distributions of interval level data. When the distribution is extremely skewed and if it contains ordinal level data, the mode may be a better choice.

5   If further statistical measures are to be considered, the mean should be preferred.

6   If a quick but rough measure is needed, the mode should be computed.

7   If information about the central trend is wanted, the mean is the best choice

8   If information is wanted about the location of cases in the two halves of the distribution, the median is a better measure.

Inferential Statistics

Inferential statistics are basically statistics which allow us to draw inferences about a population from which the sample was drawn. According to Dometrius [1992: 171] "These inferences are never absolute declarations that the population parameter must be a certain value or contained within a range of values. Instead, they are probability statements, statements that have a high probability of being true for the population." Inferential statistics are commonly used in hypothesis testing. Statisticians and researchers have developed a number of statistical techniques and tests which help us to test these hypotheses from a variety of sample and population distributions. Two of the most commonly used statistical tests are the t-test and chi-square. The t-test is a parametric statistic while the chi-square is a non-parametric statistic. Parametric statistics require the characteristics studied to be normally distributed in the specified population and the variables measured intervally (e.g. examination score). On the other hand, non-parametric statistics do not require the characteristics studied to be normally distributed in the specified population and variables can be measured ordinally or nominally (e.g. type of religion).

● The t-test is used to test differences between two means from independent samples. To conduct a t-test the researcher requires random samples. In the case of a single sample measured twice, the data should be intervally scaled and normally distributed with equal population variances.

- The chi-square test is used to compare two or more independent samples. It also requires the samples to be randomly drawn from a population. However, unlike the t-test, it is used for nominal variables. In other words, the researcher requires frequencies to conduct a chi-square test.

Because so many of the variables used by social researchers are nominally scaled, the chi-square is perhaps the most popularly used test of significance in social research. Below is an example of how to use chi-square.

Chi-square

The chi-square statistic focuses directly on how close the observed frequencies are to what they are expected to be (represented by the expected frequencies) under the null hypothesis. Based on just the observed and expected frequencies,

$$\chi^2 = \Sigma \frac{(o-e)^2}{e}$$

$$e = \frac{(row\ margin\ total)(column\ margin\ total)}{N}$$

o = the obtained frequency in any cell
e = the expected frequency in any cell
χ^2 = computed value of chi-square

Let us test a hypothesis using chi-square. Suppose we had the following hypotheses:

Null hypothesis: The proportion of students in Irvine Hall who listen to reggae music is the same as the proportion of students on Taylor Hall who listen to reggae music.

Research hypothesis: The proportion of students in Irvine Hall who listen to reggae music is not the same as the proportion of students in Taylor Hall who listen to reggae music.

Step 1 Arrange the data in the form of a 2x2 table.

	Irvine	Taylor	
Listen to reggae	12	8	20
Do not listen to reggae	6	16	22
	18	24	N=42

Step 2 Obtain expected frequency for each cell.

	Irvine	Taylor	
	12 (8.57)	8 (11.43)	20
	6 (9.43)	16 (12.57)	22
	18	24	N=42

$$\text{Upper-left } e = \frac{(20)(18)}{42} = \frac{360}{42} = 8.57$$

$$\text{Upper-right } e = \frac{(20)(24)}{42} = \frac{480}{42} = 11.43$$

$$\text{Lower-left } e = \frac{(22)(18)}{42} = \frac{396}{42} = 9.43$$

$$\text{Lower-right } e = \frac{(22)(24)}{42} = \frac{528}{42} = 12.57$$

Step 3 Subtract the expected frequencies from the observed frequencies $o - e$.

(Upper-left)	$12 - 8.57 = 3.43$
(Upper-right)	$8 - 11.43 = -3.43$
(Lower-left)	$6 - 9.43 = -3.43$
(Lower-right)	$16 - 12.57 = 3.43$

Step 4 Square the difference $(o - e)^2$

Upper-left	$(3.43)^2 = 11.76$
Upper-right	$(-3.43)^2 = 11.76$
Lower-left	$(-3.43)^2 = 11.76$
Lower-right	$(3.43)^2 = 11.76$

Step 5 Divide by the expected frequency

(Upper-left)	$\dfrac{11.76}{8.57} = 1.37$
(Upper-right)	$\dfrac{11.76}{11.43} = 1.03$
(Lower-left)	$\dfrac{11.76}{9.43} = 1.25$
(Lower-right)	$\dfrac{11.76}{12.56} = 0.94$

Step 6 Sum these quotients $\Sigma \frac{(o-e)^2}{e}$

$$\begin{array}{r} 1.37 \\ 1.03 \\ 1.25 \\ \underline{0.94} \\ \chi^2 = 4.59 \end{array}$$

Step 7 Find degrees of freedom (number of rows minus 1 multiplied by number of columns minus 1).

$$\begin{aligned} df \ &= (r - 1)\,(c - 1) \\ &= (2 - 1)\,(2 - 1) \\ &= (1)\,(1) \end{aligned}$$

Step 8 Compare the observed chi-square value with the appropriate chi-square value in Appendix 4.

$$\text{Observed } \chi^2 = 4.59$$
$$\text{Table } \chi^2 = 3.84$$
$$df = 1$$
$$\chi = .05$$

Conclusion

Based on the fact that the obtained value is larger than the table value, we reject the null hypothesis and conclude that the proportion of students in Irvine Hall who listen to reggae music is not the same as the proportion of students in Taylor Hall who listen to reggae music.

A note of caution

In cases where the expected frequencies are smaller than ten for 2x2 tables, a modified formula, using Yates Correction, should be employed. That formula is:

$$\chi^2 = \Sigma \frac{(|o-e|-.50)^2}{e}$$

Correlation

Correlation refers to the strength and direction of the relationship between two variables. Correlation analysis is usually employed in bivariate analysis. Bivariate refers to a relationship between two variables. For example, we can use a correlation coefficient to indicate the strength and direction of a relationship between socio-economic status and education. The strength would tell us if the relationship is strong or weak while the direction would tell us whether the relationship is positive or negative. Correlation coefficients usually range between –1.00 and +1.00. A perfect negative relationship is indicated by –1.00 and perfect positive relationship by +1.00. If in a research project we found that the correlation between socio-economic status and education was + .60 we would conclude that there was a relatively strong positive relationship between the two variables. In other words, as a person's education increases his or her socio-economic status is likely to improve. On the other hand, if the coefficient was –.60, we would conclude that there was a relatively strong negative relationship between socio-economic status and education. That is to say, as education improves social status will tend to worsen. Keep in mind that negative is not the same as no relationship. No relationship is just that, zero correlation.

The correlation coefficient used should be a function of the level of measurement of the variables. We first have to determine whether our variables are measured nominally, ordinally or intervally before doing a correlation analysis. Here is a list of some popular correlation coefficients and the types of variables with which they should be used.

1. Pearson's r (used to detect linear relationships): Variables should be measured intervally.

2. Gamma: Both variables should be ordinal or rank ordered.

3. Spearman's rank-order correlation or Rho: Both variables should be ordinal or rank ordered.

4. Phi: The variables should be nominal and the data should be cast in the form of a two by two (2x2) table. This refers to two rows and two columns. For instance, if we were studying the relationship between sex and heart attacks we could divide both variables into two categories each. That is, the variable 'sex' = 'male' or 'female'; and 'health status' = 'good' or 'bad'.

5. Cramer's V: Cramer's V is used when we have tables larger than two rows and two columns. For example, if we were investigating the relation between religion and education we might divide religion into three categories and education into four categories to give us a 3x4 table.

Tables and Social Research

In research we use tables on many occasions. If we conduct survey type research we are concerned with presenting the data in a manner which is easy to understand. Tables, like graphs and charts, do a great deal to lessen the tediousness of pages of written text and invariably help to bring across the message. Whether in the field of education, social sciences, medical sciences or nursing education, tables are an integral part of any report presentation.

When we design a table the intent is to accomplish two goals simultaneously. We seek to simply communicate the findings and, at the same time, allow the readers to interpret the findings for themselves. Not all data go in a table. We therefore have to choose what should be represented, perhaps leaving some additional information to be presented in an appendix.

Types of tables

We can consider the types of tables from the point of view of usage. There are two types:

1. General or reference tables

2. Summary or text tables

General or reference tables (see Table 10.5)

Table 10.5 represents the production of bananas in three selected parishes. Production is reported in thousands and for specific years, namely 1980, 1983, 1986, 1989 and 1992. From the table we can read that for the year 1980, parish A had the highest production of bananas for the three parishes. Its production of 100,000 exceeded that of parish C by 20,000 and production of parish B by 50,000. Parish A remained the major producer of bananas from 1980 to 1992.

Table 10.5 Production of bananas in specific years by selected parishes

Years	Production in Parishes ('000s)		
	Parish A	Parish B	Parish C
1980	100	50	80
1983	146	50	90
1986	245	90	130
1989	400	250	270
1992	480	330	350

We commonly find these types of tables in texts representing some source data or information. These tables can also be termed percentage tables as, frequently, the researcher uses simple percentages in addition to the raw numbers. Examples of these are census data (table showing total population by gender by special area), or a straightforward frequency distribution (percentage of homes burgled in selected rural districts), and monthly clinic or school attendance statistics. The emphasis is on clarity so that information can be found. As there is no special distinction between the variables in terms of placement, some of these tables, for example, census data or statistical reports, can become quite complicated. Sometimes these tables are used for comparison, that is comparison across columns or categories. In those cases the use of ratios, percentages, averages or other computed relationships is preferred.

Summary or text tables (see Table 10.6)

In comparison to the above, these tables are relatively small and usually refer to some survey finding as in contingency tables, for example. These tables are computed from a raw data source and usually aggregate data in some fashion. They are normally accompanied by some discussion of the findings in the text. Contingency tables are sometimes referred to as cross-tabulation tables. As a rule, they use nominal or ordinal level data and reflect the data from bivariate or multivariate studies. Data in a contingency table are arranged in cells made by the intersection of rows and columns. Let us look at Table 10.6.

Table 10.6 Relationship between weight and susceptibility to heart attack

Stub	Box Heading		
Men	Have experienced a heart attack	Have not had a heart attack	Total
Overweight	400	100	500
Underweight	100	400	500
Total	500	500	1000

There are nine cells: four of these contain the observed frequencies while the totals are described as marginals. This would be called a 2x2 table having two rows (horizontal and usually the dependent variable) and two columns (upright and usually the independent variable). Data in each cell therefore represent both variables.

Constructing a table

There are four essential parts of a table. These are:

1. Title: identifies the information which the table wishes to communicate; and states the information which the table contains

2. Stub: left-hand column with its headings and sub-headings

3. Box heading: headings of the other columns across the top

4. Body: cell contents; the information that is recorded in each cell

The title of a table should make it clear what information is being communicated. It should be the first thing that the reader looks at. The title should therefore:

● summarize the contents

- identify objects of the research
- where nessary indicate the nature of the values being used in the cells, that is percentages, means or raw numbers

Do not use mnemonics (for example, 'STRUCR' means 'Roof of Structure') from a computer printout as you may be the only one who knows what it means. Similarly, when reporting on opinion polls always use the actual question as the title of the table so that everyone will know what you are talking about. It is much easier to understand 'Which of the present deputies would you like to see as prime minister?' as opposed to 'Views on possible succession to the present prime minister'.

In order to construct Table 10.6 we ran a survey on a sample of men in an attempt to see if there was any relationship between body weight and whether or not they had experienced a heart attack. We separated the responses into those who were or were not overweight and then counted the responses to see whether or not they had experienced a heart attack. Just because these men are fat and they do have heart attacks does not mean that it is the excess weight that causes the attack. We have to be very careful in our interpretation of contingency tables, as we are never speaking about cause, but rather association or relationship. It could well be that the attack was brought on by the types of foods they ate or perhaps they had an early attack and decided to eat whatever they wished, whenever they wished.

When we speak of cells we are referring to the intersection between rows and columns. As in everyday life, columns are upright while rows fall horizontally. Therefore, cell (a) in the body of the table is that position where 400 of the 500 overweight men had experienced a heart attack. Note this cell does not simply indicate that 400 men had experienced a heart attack: it is more specific than that. It tells us that 400 of the 500 men who had experienced a heart attack were overweight. Cells with missing data are just as important and should be included as blanks or non-response.

These tables can become quite complex as you may wish to add row percentages, column percentages or total percentages. In each case, the type of percentage reflects the total used in its computation. For example, row percentages use the row total (total at the end of the row) for its computation while column percentages use the column total (total at the end of the column).

Be careful in rounding figures as you might then find that totals do not compute. Percentages should add up to 100. Where this does not occur, some explanation should be given. At times you might wish to use whole numbers and indicate in the headings that they are really thousands, for example, ('000).

Table 10.5 is built from raw data. It presents the number of bananas (in thousands) produced in each parish in each year identified. Here again you could use percentages to bring out the findings. You should be careful, however, not to use percentages inappropriately. Frequently, where numbers are small it might be better to use ratios.

There is some discussion about the placement of independent and dependent variables. Although there is no hard and fast rule, for clarity reports tend to have the independent variables across the top with the categories in the box headings (as in Table 10.5, parish is the independent variable as it is possible that changes in production may be related to climatic conditions). What is important to remember is that if the independent variable is across the top, then the table should compute percentages by columns. It is always easier to compare columns, especially those which are side by side. Remember, the axis containing the dependent variable should not have any additional independent or controlled variables.

Tables may also have footnotes explaining some particular feature. For example, you may have data from a sample with varying values in different cells. The footnote may explain this as well as indicate the method of sampling used. Often, also, you will find a properly referenced source (including year, place of publication and page number or range) indicated at the bottom of the table, as in many cases the table is not original to the text but included from some other source. Naturally, tables may also have subheadings in the box headings.

Nowadays we have word-processing packages which create tables with ease. It then becomes the researcher's choice whether or not to have side lines, double lines between headings and titles in bold. Whatever the choice, we must ensure that the format remains consistent throughout the text.

Main Points

📖 Having collected, cleaned and edited the data, the next stages in the research process are analysis and presentation. Analysis refers to summarizing observations, testing hypotheses, computing statistics and arriving at conclusions. Presentation involves organizing data in an interpretable form. These forms include graphs, tables and summary statistics.

📖 Types of graphic presentations are bar charts, pie charts, line graphs and frequency polygons.

📖 There are two types of statistics, descriptive and inferential. Descriptive statistics are computations which help to organize and describe characteristics of large samples (for example, mean, mode, median). Inferential statistics allow us to make conclusions about a population based on the sample from which it was drawn (for example, t-test, F-test and chi-square).

📖 Correlation refers to the strength and direction of the relationship between two variables. Correlation analysis is used mainly in bivariable analysis.

📖 The type of correlation coefficient that is employed in a study depends on the level of measurement used. For example, variables measured on an interval scale should use the Pearson Correlation Coefficient, whereas nominally scaled variables would use either Cramer's V or Phi.

📖 There are two types of tables – general or reference, and summary or text. General tables simply provide source data or information. Summary tables usually display survey findings in the form of contingency or cross-tabulation analysis.

1. Use a pie chart to depict the following data:

Faculty of Student	f	%
Social Sciences	80	40
Natural Sciences	60	30
Medical Sciences	20	10
Engineering	40	20
Total	200	100

2. Use a bar graph to depict the following data:

	Sex	
Faculty of Student	Male	Female
Social Sciences	30	50
Natural Sciences	35	25
Medical Sciences	10	10
Engineering	25	15
Total	100	100

3. A random sample of 134 students at the University of the West Indies was asked whether or not they were in favour of a political union of Caricom. Using the data presented in the table below test the hypothesis that: Education level of parent does not affect student's preference for political union.

	Education Level of Parent	
Response	Tertiary	No Tertiary
Favour Political Union	46	34
Opposed to Political Union	26	28
Total	72	62

| Chapter Eleven | The Ethics of Social Research |

The dilemma which the social researcher faces is that of collecting valid and reliable information from human subjects without infringing on their personal rights and freedoms. Even greater than this, however, is the humbling fact that the researcher is sometimes faced with the possibility of inflicting psychological or emotional harm as a consequence of the research.

We are now past the hurdle of feeling that the acquisition of knowledge is the only guiding principle for good research or that subjects are simply there to furnish any information the researcher requires. Never mind how 'captured' the respondents may be (for example, inmates of a state prison or a concentration camp), the researcher is now bound to consider the eventual consequences of the research design. A symbol of unethical research is the Tuskegee Syphilis Study, also called 'Bad Blood'. Until the 1970s, when a newspaper report caused a scandal to erupt, the USA Public Health Service sponsored a study in which poor, uneducated black men in an Alabama prison suffered and died of untreated syphilis, while researchers studied the severe physical disabilities that appear in advanced stages of the disease. Despite their unethical treatment of the subjects, the researchers were allowed to publish their results for some forty years.

Unfortunately, maintenance of a moral stance is easier to express in texts than to ensure in the field. As a consequence there have been efforts in the USA since 1974 (for example, National Research Act, Public Law 93–348, National Association of Social Workers Code of Ethics 1980, Code of Ethics of the American Sociological Association) that have attempted to identify unacceptable practices and procedures. We have also seen a range of review boards at educational and research institutions being established. However, the responsibility remains with you, the researcher.

The researcher should reflect on research actions and consult his or her conscience, weighing this against personal deep-seated values and beliefs. "If values are to be taken seriously, they cannot be expressed and laid aside but must instead be guides to action for the sociologist. They determine who will be investigated, for what purpose and in whose service" [Sagarin 1973: 63].

Ethical considerations result in curtailing specific bits and types of research. These considerations have also impacted on the use made of research, with limitations being placed on implementation and a widening of potential readership.

It is generally agreed that subjects, as people, should have the right to decide whether or not they will participate in the process. This right to self-determination deserves to be further examined.

Voluntary consent and informed consent

Individuals should always have the right to decide whether or not he or she wishes to take part in the research. In order to ensure this, the researcher should explain the intent of the project. This is *informed consent*, that is the respondent is informed about that which he or she is consenting to be a part of. This will include statements such as research intent and use of findings, identification of interviewer, sample size and method of selection, guarantees of anonymity and confidentiality and commitment to provide summary of findings. However, a respondent may volunteer to become part of the research process without fully understanding the purpose or repercussions of the research. This is known as *voluntary consent*.

Many times, however, people appear to be volunteers when, really, they are not. For example, students in a classroom, or clients in a social service agency may participate in a study out of feelings of obligation. The researcher in these instances should never force anyone to participate. In some situations, where there is little risk of harm to subjects, for example, in the use of two-way mirrors in educational research, proceeding should not cause embarrassment or necessitate individualized permission.

Deception

Never lie about the research intent. Lying includes deception, as well as any attempt to disguise the research, and to use covert research methods. There are times when the researcher may misrepresent his or her intent in order to gain entry or to prevent modification of behaviour. Deception, however, is not preferable to honesty. If one finds it necessary to use deception then they should secure some form of signed consent, perhaps after the research has been completed.

Another side of deception refers to the researcher producing incorrect results intentionally. At times this might occur in an attempt to secure necessary funding or desired approbation. This type of deception calls into question the scientific integrity assumed in the choice of research design.

Privacy, anonymity and confidentiality – PAC(T)

This PAC(T) really refers to the maintenance of self-respect in both respondent and researcher. In participating in a piece of research, respondents should never have to wonder if someone else knows what they have said confidentially, if someone somewhere is discussing particular preferences or details of past behaviours. Researchers by design plan to invade respondents' privacy of beliefs, as well as the most intimate details of behaviour. The problem arises when respondents may be spied on in 'public' settings using covert research, disguise, periscopes and other such devices in an attempt to gather 'private' data.

Anonymity and confidentiality are more serious issues than simply a question of whether one's name is recorded or not. For example, in ethnographic studies, one may alter a respondent's name and confuse a few details between respondents. This helps to ensure anonymity. However, anonymity can never be totally guaranteed in a face-to-face interview since the interviewer may be able to identify a given response with a particular respondent. Confidentiality, however, means that "information may have names attached to it, but the researcher holds it in confidence or keeps it secret from the public" [Newman 1991: 448].

To ensure anonymity and confidentiality researchers tend to reduce inform-ation to numerical codes and statistical aggregates. In this way, anonymity is quickly assured early in the data analysis process. It also means that where reports are made, the audience reacts to percentages and bar charts rather than specific individuals' views.

Particularly in small samples or small villages or communities where people know each other well, the twin issues of anonymity and confidentiality assume great importance.

Other harm to subjects

At times the topic of the research can generate feelings of anxiety, stress or even fear in the respondent. It is incumbent on the researcher to be aware of this in the design and build in safeguards to combat this. These may include choice of methodology, choice of interviewer or debriefing after the session. One has to be careful not to leave the respondent anxious on completion of the exercise – anxious as to the outcome, wondering if they gave the 'right' responses or anxious at the new feelings surfacing as a consequence of the interview. The potential for harm is enormous.

Ethics and survey research

When reporting survey research findings there are a few points to bear in mind which will dispel a great deal of the distrust which the reader may be having [Newman 1991: 271].

A note on bias. The question of bias attends every step of the research process. Whether it be with question design, sampling assumptions or even choice of theories seen as relevant to analysis, researchers need to bear in mind the impact of bias as a real functioning limitation. Bias can enter the process through the kinds of questions asked, the wording of questions or the ways respondents are required to answer. For example, the government is desirous of eradicating blight from the inner-city ghettos. The first step is data gathering which will both describe the socio-demographic characteristics of the community as well as identify the needs of the community. At the same time, however, the researcher might be using the community mapping to become more knowledgeable about the community and its people. Perhaps this researcher feels that all ghetto residents carry guns and that, drug 'Dons' rule the roost. This bias may well temper the approach made to the people in the ghetto and even the types of questions asked. Attempts to probe are likely to end up putting words in people's mouths.

When analysing the data the researcher may be unintentionally careless, introducing errors of calculation or interpretation. Especially where major policy decisions are to be made, this kind of bias can be far-reaching in its consequences.

Gunnar Myrdal in his book *The Asian Drama: an Enqiiry into the Poverty of Nations* [1973] dedicated one entire volume to the question of the implications and ethical considerations cf foreign aid to developing countries, suggesting that ethnocentrism and cultural bias do affect the process of aid. For us in developing countries, we need to bear in mind the source of the report as we attempt to implement recommendations. Too frequently, researchers feel that their assumptions are the only right ones and preference for any other way of thinking merely reflects lack of knowledge and/or experience.

Researchers who are engaged in research across cultures need to be constantly on the alert, learning the nuances of the other culture, and becoming aware of how their own culture influences and biases their own thinking.

Main Points

In any piece of research, ethical considerations should be at the forefront of the researcher's mind, influencing both conceptualization and design. Fundamentally, the intent of the researcher is to try to gain valid information without infringing on anyone's rights or privacy or even more critically, harming the individual, agency or community.

The researcher should always be guided by some kind of moral principle in the design of the research which will ensure honesty on his or her behalf.

In research, the main ethical concerns are to ensure voluntary consent and informed consent. Respondents should always be aware of the research intent and their freedom to refuse inclusion in the process, should the desire/need arise.

📖 Researchers should try to steer away from deception and ensure privacy, anonymity and confidentiality of respondents and their responses.

📖 Use of research findings is also dictated by ethical considerations, bearing in mind all of the above.

Exercise

A familiar scenario

The government of a Caribbean island, Carbani, decides to solicit funding for a low income housing project with the intention of providing housing for a select group of urban residents. It already has a good relationship with an overseas government. This overseas government when approached expresses willingness to assist – projecting a two-year start-up date. This will necessitate a group of low-income housing experts coming to Carbani to conduct a feasibility study. Permission is granted.

Experts arrive in Carbani, first-time visitors to the Caribbean. They intend to stay one week on a preliminary visit, then return in five weeks' time to conduct a feasibility study. During the preliminary visit, contact is made with the appropriate ministry; the projected housing site is visited and a tour is made of Carbani.

Experts return to Carbani and request:

1. Local interviewers.

2. Basic relevant statistical information.

They conduct training of local interviewers in use of the instrument designed by experts to access information from the select group of urban residents. Interviewers are given IDs with their names and name of the local government ministry. They are also advised that if asked, they may let respondents know that the ministry is planning to build new housing in the area soon. It is also emphasized that housing addresses and, if possible, the first name of the respondent, should always be recorded as a supervisory check will be made. Training is conducted by experts and interviewers are all experienced persons.

Can you identify potential points of

(a)   ethical misconduct on the part of both government agencies and foreign experts; and

(b)   negative influences on the research process?

How to Review a Scientific Article

I. Conceptualization

   A. Research Area or Problem – What is the research problem or general area of research?

      • A problem is an interrogative statement that asks: What relationship exists between two or more variables? The answer to this research problem is what is being sought in the research.

   B. Most Pertinent Literature – Who does the author list as the major references?

      • Cite the most important sources you think influenced the researcher's study. You can find authors' names within the text of the article, in footnotes as well as at the end in references or in the bibliography.

   C. Major Concepts Defined – What are the major concepts/variables used by the researcher, and how does he or she define them?

      • A concept is an abstract idea like prejudice or achievement or intelligence.

   D. Basic Hypothesis: Major Concepts (Variables) Related – A hypothesis is a conjectural statement of the relation between two or more variables. Hypotheses are always in declarative sentence form, and they relate either generally or specifically, variables to variables.

      • Diagram the relationship between these variables at the most general level used by the other $V_T \longrightarrow V_D$.

   E. Sub-hypotheses:

      • Diagram the relationship between specific independent and dependent variables.

      • An independent variable is the presumed cause of the dependent variable.

      • You predict from the independent variable to the dependent variable.

   F. Operational Definitions:

      • An operational definition assigns meaning to a concept or a variable by specifying the activities or 'operations' necessary to measure it. Do such and such in this and that manner.

      • Operationalization refers simply to a specification of the steps, procedures, or operations that you will go through in actually measuring and identifying the variables you want to observe.

II. Research Design:

   A. Technique of Observation:

   1. Instrument: What is the method of observation?

      • The instrument is the technique or tool used by the researcher for measuring observation, i.e. survey, questionnaire and case studies.

2. Reliability: Is the research replicable? If the research was repeated would we get the same results? Are there errors of measurement in the study?

3. Validity: How valid is the study? Did the researcher measure what he or she set out to measure? And, is this research generalizable to other settings and times?

B. Design of Proof:

How close does the researcher's method or research design come to the ideal of the scientific method?

C. Sample:

1. Size: (Adequate?) How many people are in the sample? Is this sample size large enough to generalize to the entire population?

2. Method of Selection: How are people selected to be in the sample? Are they chosen randomly, where every person studied has an equal chance of being in the sample, or are they specially selected, e.g. friends, etc.

III. **Implementation of Research:**

A. Collection of Data: (time, place, by whom, etc.)

Does the author specify when, where, and by whom the observations were collected?

B. Data Processing Techniques:

What steps did the researcher go through in the preparation of his or her data for presentation? Is there any mention of coding and tabulating procedures?

C. Presentation of Data:

Method: How does the researcher present the data in the article? Are there tables, graphs or percentages?

3. Levels of Generalization: What does the author say about the level of generalization which may be safely assumed in the context of the research design? If we substitute other variables in the model, will the results still be correct?

D. Findings:

Do the data presented in the article clearly support the original hypotheses?

E. Explanation of Deviance:

Does the author explain why some of the results vary or deviate from the original hypotheses? Why did the researcher not get the expected results?

Conclusions

1. Basic hypothesis supported? If hypothesis not supported does the author explain why?

2. Suggestions for further research?

- What are the areas for further research? Do the results lead to questions that the author does not mention? What are they?

3. Is the research well presented? Is it also convincing?

[Reproduced with the permission of Frank A. Santopolo, Colorado State University, Colorado, USA]

Appendix 2

Some Essential Tasks for Completing a Research Project

Many students who are new to social research do not realize that a research project demands a great deal of organization of essential tasks which must be assigned to various individuals on the research team. Writing the research proposal is one thing, implementing it is another. This list of tasks will help your team to complete its project in a more orderly fashion.

- Revise your problem statement so that you know your objective.
- Work on your sample design and the procedure you will use to collect your data.
- Construct questions for each sub-problem.
- Develop coding instructions for each question. (Remember precoded or post-coding strategies.)
- Construct dummy tables for each question.
- Construct dummy table for anticipated cross-tabulation of variables [Q2 (Attributes) x Q4 (Attitudes)].
- Review, revise, eliminate, add questions to accomplish objective.
- Integrate all questions into most logical order to complete the questionnaire construction.
- Write introductory statement for questionnaire. One must explain the purpose of the study and what you expect the respondent to do.
- Test questionnaire on some people who are not members of your team.
- Revise questionnaire if necessary.
- Type questionnaire on ditto/stencil master.
- Print, collate and staple questionnaire.
- Distribute questionnaires to sample population.
- Collect questionnaires.
- Number questionnaires as received.
- Evaluate each questionnaire returned for usability. Tabulate responses by tables previously constructed.
- Analyse tables.
- Write up analysis for each table.
- Reflect on your findings.
- Integrate analyses guided by content of original research problem and sub-problems. (Answer the basic research questions.)
- The review of the literature and the methods sections can be written while the above tasks are in process.

Literature review

○ Aim at presenting between 8 and 15 studies which actually gave you understanding of the theoretical and/or methical problems you faced doing your project.

○ It does not often take much more than three to five sentences to review a piece of literature. For instance, "Professor X studied the eating patterns of college students by having the participants keep a seven-day diary. He found that students on hall ate more nutritionally balanced meals than students who lived in other types of residences."

○ There are several ways to organize and present this review.
1. By date of publication. Oldest first.
2. By hypotheses or sub-problems.
3. By theory and methods.

● Write the methods section. Describe the procedures used. What worked, what didn't. Be thorough but concise.

● Write first draft of final report. Critique the draft. Rewrite the draft. Are you satisfied?

● Type final report. Check typed report.

● Present final report.

As you can see, this project cannot be completed overnight, or even in a week of nights. But it can be done, and has been done with proper time management and the cooperation of each team member within the semester schedule. In the real world work situation you will be asked to do things that will call on the skills and knowledge you have learnt in this exercise. Profit by this experience by giving it the proper priority.

[Reproduced with the permission of Frank A. Santopolo, Colorado State University, Colorado, USA]

Appendix 3

Table of Random Digits

00000	10097	32533	76520	13586	34673	54876	80959	09117	39292
00001	37542	04805	64894	74296	24805	24037	20636	10402	00822
00002	08422	68953	19645	09303	23209	02560	15953	34764	35080
00003	99019	02529	09376	70715	38311	31165	88676	74397	04436
00004	12807	99970	80157	36147	64032	36653	98951	16877	12171
00005	66065	74717	34072	76850	36697	36170	65813	39885	11199
00006	31060	10805	45571	82406	35303	42614	86799	07439	23403
00007	85269	77602	02051	65692	68665	74818	73053	85247	18623
00008	63573	32135	05325	47048	90553	57548	28468	28709	83491
00009	73796	45753	03529	64778	35808	34282	60935	20344	35273
00010	98520	17767	14905	68607	22109	40558	60970	93433	50500
00011	11805	05431	39808	27732	50725	68248	29405	24201	52775
00012	83452	99634	06288	98083	13746	70078	18475	40610	68711
00013	88685	40200	86507	58401	36766	67951	90364	76493	29609
00014	99594	67348	87517	64969	91826	08928	93785	61368	23478
00015	65481	17674	17468	50950	58047	76974	73039	57186	40218
00016	80124	35635	17727	08015	45318	22374	21115	78253	14385
00017	74350	99817	77402	77214	43236	00210	45521	64237	96286
00018	69916	26803	66252	29148	36936	87203	76621	13990	94400
00019	09893	20505	14225	68514	46427	56788	96297	78822	54382
00020	91499	14523	68479	27686	46162	83554	94750	89923	37089
00021	80336	94598	26940	36858	70297	34135	53140	33340	42050
00022	44104	81949	85157	47954	32979	26575	57600	40881	22222
00023	12550	73742	11100	02040	12860	74697	96644	89439	28707
00024	63606	49329	16505	34484	40219	52563	43651	77082	07207
00025	61196	90446	26457	47774	51924	33729	65394	59593	42582
00026	15474	45266	95270	79953	59367	83848	82396	10118	33211
00027	94557	28573	67897	54387	54622	44431	91190	42592	92927
00028	42481	16213	97344	08721	16868	48767	03071	12059	25701
00029	23523	78317	73208	89837	68935	91416	26252	29663	05522
00030	04493	52494	75246	33824	45862	51025	61962	79335	65337
00031	00549	97654	64051	88159	96119	63896	54692	82391	23287
00032	35963	15307	26898	09354	33351	35462	77974	50024	90103
00033	59808	08391	45427	26842	83609	49700	13021	24892	78565
00034	46058	85236	01390	92286	77281	44077	93910	83647	70617
00035	32179	00597	87379	25241	05567	07007	86743	17157	85394
00036	69234	61406	20117	45204	15956	60000	18743	92423	97118
00037	19565	41430	01758	75379	40419	21585	66674	36806	84962
00038	45155	14938	19476	07246	43667	94543	59047	90033	20826
00039	94864	31994	36168	10851	34888	81553	01540	35456	05014

Appendix 4

Chi square Distribution*

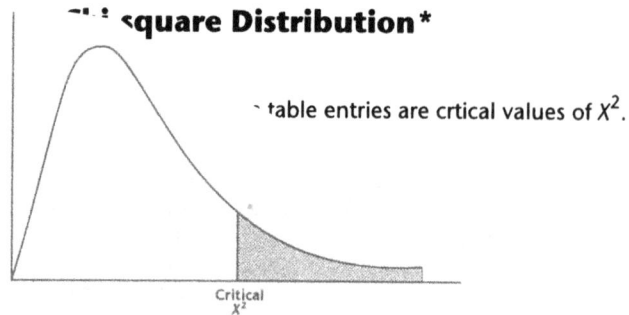

table entries are crtical values of X^2.

df	Proportion in Critical Region				
	0.10	0.05	0.025	0.01	0.005
1	2.71	3.84	5.02	6.63	7.88
2	4.61	5.99	7.38	9.21	10.60
3	6.25	7.81	9.35	11.34	12.84
4	7.78	9.49	11.14	13.28	14.86
5	9.24	11.07	12.83	15.09	16.75
6	10.64	12.59	14.45	16.81	18.55
7	12.02	14.07	16.01	18.48	20.28
8	13.36	15.51	17.53	20.09	21.96
9	14.68	16.92	19.02	21.67	23.59
10	15.99	18.31	20.48	23.21	25.19
11	17.28	19.68	21.92	24.72	26.76
12	18.55	21.03	23.34	26.22	28.30
13	19.81	22.36	24.74	27.69	29.82
14	21.06	23.68	26.12	29.14	31.32
15	22.31	25.00	27.49	30.58	32.80
16	23.54	26.30	28.85	32.00	34.27
17	24.77	27.59	30.19	33.41	35.72
18	25.99	28.87	31.53	34.81	37.16
19	27.20	30.14	32.85	36.19	38.58
20	28.41	31.41	34.17	37.57	40.00
21	29.62	32.67	35.48	38.93	41.40
22	30.81	33.92	36.78	40.29	42.80
23	32.01	35.17	38.08	41.64	44.18
24	33.20	36.42	39.36	42.98	45.56
25	34.38	37.65	40.65	44.31	46.93
26	35.56	38.89	41.92	45.64	48.29
27	36.74	40.11	43.19	46.96	49.64
28	37.92	41.34	44.46	48.28	50.99
29	39.09	42.56	45.72	49.59	52.34
30	40.26	43.77	46.98	50.89	53.67
40	51.81	55.76	59.34	63.69	66.77
50	63.17	67.50	71.42	76.15	79.49
60	74.40	79.08	83.30	88.38	91.95
70	85.53	90.53	95.02	100.42	104.22
80	96.58	101.88	106.63	112.33	116.32
90	107.56	113.14	118.14	124.12	128.30
100	118.50	124.34	129.56	135.81	140.17

Introduction to Social Research

Appendix 5

Excerpt from the Code of Ethics, American Sociological Association*

Research

I. THE PRACTICE OF SOCIOLOGY

A. Objectivity and Integrity.

Sociologists should strive to maintain objectivity and integrity in the conduct of sociological research and practice.

A.1. Sociologists should adhere to the highest possible technical standards in their research, teaching and practice.

A.2. Since individual sociologists vary in their research modes, skills, and experience, sociologists should always set forth *ex ante* the limits of their knowledge and the disciplinary and personal limitations that condition the validity of findings which affect whether or not a research project can be successfully completed.

A.4. In presenting their work, sociologists are obligated to report their findings fully and should not misrepresent the findings of their research. When work is presented, they are obligated to report their findings fully and without omission of significant data. To the best of their ability, sociologists should also disclose details of their theories, methods and research designs that might bear upon interpretations of research findings.

A.5. Sociologists must report fully all sources of financial support in their publications and must note any special relations to any sponsor.

A.6. Sociologists should not make any guarantees to respondents, individuals, groups or organizations – unless there is full intention and ability to honor such commitments. All such guarantees, once made, must be honored.

A.8. Sociologists should provide adequate information and citations concerning scales and other measures used in their research.

A.9. Sociologists must not accept such grants, contracts or research assignments as appear likely to require violation of the principles enunciated in this Code, and should dissociate themselves from research when they discover a violation and are unable to achieve its correction.

A.10. When financial support for a project has been accepted, sociologists must make every reasonable effort to complete the proposed work on schedule, including reports to the funding source.

A.11. When several sociologists, including students, are involved in joint projects, there should be mutually accepted explicit agreements at the outset with respect to division of work, compensation, access to data, rights of authorship, and other rights and responsibilities. Such agreements may need to be modified as the project evolves and such modifications must be agreed upon jointly.

B. Disclosure and Respect for the Rights of Research Populations.

Disparities in wealth, power, and social status between the sociologist and respondents and clients may reflect and create problems of equity in research collaboration. Conflict of interest for the sociologist may occur in research and practice. Also to follow the precepts of the scientific method – such as those requiring full disclosure – may entail adverse consequences or personal risks for individuals and groups. Finally, irresponsible actions by a single researcher or research team can eliminate or reduce future access to a category of respondents by the entire profession and its allied fields.

B.1.　Sociologists should not misuse their positions as professional social scientists for fraudulent purposes or as a pretext for gathering intelligence for any organization or government. Sociologists should not mislead respondents involved in a research project as to the purpose for which the research is being conducted.

B.4.　The process of conducting sociological research must not expose respondents to substantial risk of personal harm. Informed consent must be obtained when the risks of research are greater than the risks of everyday life. Where modest risk or harm is anticipated, informed consent must be obtained.

B.5.　Sociologists should take culturally appropriate steps to secure informed consent and to avoid invasions of privacy. Special actions may be necessary where the individuals studied are illiterate, have very low social status, or are unfamiliar with social research.

B.6.　To the extent possible in a given study sociologists should anticipate potential threats to confidentiality. Such means as the removal of identifiers, the use of randomized responses and other statistical solutions to problems of privacy should be used where appropriate.

B.7.　Confidential information provided by research participants must be treated as such by sociologists, even when this information enjoys no legal protection or privilege and legal force is applied. The obligation to respect confidentiality also applies to members of research organizations (interviewers, coders, clerical staff, etc.) who have access to the information. It is the responsibility of administrators and chief investigators to instruct staff members on this point and to make every effort to insure that access to confidential information is restricted.

[*Extracted from Code of Ethics, American Sociological Association. Washington DC, USA]

Appendix 6

The Research Proposal: A Quick Guide

A proposal is as essential to successful research as an architect's plan is to the building of a house. Doing research cannot be left to accidental or lucky circumstances. Foresight, purposeful decision and careful consideration of important details of procedure must take place before any data gathering operation is begun. A sound proposal prevents costly errors and mistakes. Proposal writing helps to focus your thinking on important details. The proposal is not a novel. It should be written in a straightforward manner. Proposals follow a simple, logical form of presentation. The following outline is not the only arrangement that can be made of research activities, but it is the one we recommend.

   I. **The statement of the problem**

        A. The statement of the problem

        B. The sub-problems

        C. The hypotheses (if any)

        D. The limitations of the study

        E. The definitions of terms

        F. The basic assumptions

        (Examine research articles for examples)

  II. **The review of the related literature**

        Try to identify major theoretical propositions and methodological designs and/or instruments.

 III. **The data, their treatment, and their interpretation**

        A. The data

          1. The primary data (those you will collect)

          2. The secondary data (those someone else collected)

        B. The research methodology to be used (sample, instruments, etc.)

        C. The specific projected treatment of each sub-problem

          1. Sub-problem 1 (restate the sub-problem)

            a. The data needed

            b. Where the data are located

            c. How the data will be obtained

            d. How the data will be treated and interpreted

          2. Sub-problem 2 (repeat the steps for sub-problem 1)

  IV. **The importance of this study**

        (What contribution can your findings make?)

V. Identification of each project team member (Name, year, major, etc.)

VI. The selected bibliography in proper form (refer to various journals for format).

[Reproduced with the permission of Frank A. Santopolo, Colorado State University, Colorado, USA]

Glossary

Accretions – items left behind as a result of human activity.

Bar graphs – horizontally or vertically aligned graphic presentations (also called histograms) which can accommodate variables measured at any level.

Bivariate analysis – this analysis is concerned with two variables simultaneously. Most often, the data are presented in the form of contingency tables, correlations and bar charts. In a bar chart, each variable is identified by the use of a key or legend.

Chi-square – a test of significance usually used in analysing nominal level variables, and where the expected frequencies are compared against the observed ones. Chi-square is a non-parametric statistic.

Closed questions – those in a questionnaire for which the only answers accepted and recorded are those in the format of categories provided.

Coding – the assignment of numeric or alphanumeric symbols to observed verbal responses, or non-verbal communication, to facilitate data analysis.

Concept – a generalized idea about an entire class of objective phenomena.

Construct – a generalized idea about an entire class of subjective phenomena.

Content analysis – a form of unobtrusive research used by researchers to study human communication.

Contingency table – a table which represents data from two or more variables. One variable – the dependent variable – is presented in the rows while the other(s) – the independent variable(s) – is(are) presented in the columns.

Correlation – the strength and direction of the relationship between two variables.

Cross-sectional research – the study, often explanatory or descriptive, of phenomena occurring at a single particular time period.

Cumulative frequency – the sum of the frequencies for a given category and all smaller valued frequencies in that category.

Data management – the processes whereby collected data are collated, edited, coded and otherwise transformed into a form facilitating analysis and report preparation.

Depth interviewing – a semi-structured data collection method during which the researcher elicits in-depth information from the respondent in a dyadic (but occasionally triadic) conversation based on mutual understanding of honesty, openness and trust.

Descriptive statistics – statistics which help in organizing and describing data, including showing relationships between variables.

Erosions – the wearing down of items (e.g. shoes soles, foot paths, clothing) as a result of human usage or activity.

Face-to-face interviewing – a type of data collection method used in survey research during which persons from the sample population respond to questions from an interviewer, using a structured instrument, both individuals being present at the interview site.

Focus groups – one type of qualitative research, in which a fairly homogeneous group of persons, specially chosen, come together to discuss a particular topic based on a topic guide, and with guidance from a moderator, generating results which benefit from the group interaction.

Frequency distribution – a table consisting of the number of cases having the attributes of a given variable.

Hypothesis – a non-obvious statement which makes an assertion establishing a testable base about a doubtful or unknown statement.

Inferential statistics – a body of statistics that allows us to draw inferences from a sample of observations to the population from which the sample was drawn.

Informed consent – a research participant's agreement to participate in a study, after having been fully informed of the intent of the project.

Interval measure – a level of measurement describing a variable with attributes that are rank ordered with exact distances between these attributes. However, the attributes of interval measures do not have true zero points. Examples of variables with interval level measurements are IQ, measured by an examination, and temperature, measured in degrees Celsius or Fahrenheit.

Line graphs – single lines used graphically to display changes in a variable(s) or between groups over time.

Longitudinal research – the study of multiple observations made over successive time periods.

Mail interviewing – a survey data collection method which is self-administered by respondents, and which is dependent on mail services for dispatch and receipt of the questionnaire.

Mean – a measure of central tendency in which the sum of a set of scores is divided by the total number of scores.

Measurement – there are many definitions of measurement. Perhaps the simplest definition refers to the assignment of numerals or numbers to response categories of a variable. Others prefer to see measurement as the careful and purposeful observation of real world phenomena aimed at describing characteristics of a variable.

Median – a measure of central tendency referring to the middle value or middlemost point in a distribution.

Mode – a measure of central tendency referring to the most frequent or typical value in a distribution.

Moderator – person chosen for professional role of leading focus groups, based on personal characteristics such as objectivity, creativity, empathy, listening, memory and thinking skills.

Multivariate analysis – this analysis is concerned with more than two variables. For analysis, one can also use contingency or cross-tabulation tables. Multivariate tables can become quite complex.

Nominal measure – a level of measurement describing a variable which has attributes of exhaustiveness and mutual exclusiveness. Sex and religion are examples of variables with nominal level measurement.

Non-parametric test – a test of significance in which attributes of variables in a population are not normally distributed and not measured at an interval level. An example of a non-parametric test is Chi-square.

Non-probability sample – a type of sample in which there is no random selection mechanism. Examples of this type of sample include accidental sample, quota sample and snowball/mudball sample.

Null hypothesis – the hypothesis that suggests that there is no relationship between the variables under study. When the null hypothesis is rejected you 'accept' the research hypothesis.

Open-ended questions – those in a questionnaire which do not restrict the form or content of the respondents' answers, thereby allowing for the recording of elaborated verbatim responses.

Operationalization – translation of a variable into measurable terms which will remain specific for the particular piece of research.

Ordinal measure – a level of measurement in which the attributes of a variable are mutually exclusive, exhaustive and rank ordered. Social class with attributes of upper, middle and lower may be classified as an ordinal variable.

Parametric tests – tests of significance in which attributes of variables in a population are normally distributed and measured at the interval level. The t-test or t-ratio is an example of a parametric test.

Participant observation – a field-related situation in which the researcher becomes a part of the environment being measured without the community members' knowledge of the full purpose of such involvement.

Pie chart – a circular graph in which all of the slices, or sections, add up to 100 percent.

Pretesting – the process (also called 'field testing') whereby a questionnaire is administered in the field and developed through drafts to check for adequacy and accuracy.

Probability sample – a type of sample in which a random selection method is used. Examples of probability samples include simple random sample, stratified sample and systematic sample.

Probing – any expansion of the written question by the survey interviewer or focus group moderator designed to facilitate comprehension and/or response by the respondent(s) in the data collection process.

Qualitative research – an approach to data gathering which comprises in-depth investigation of human perceptions, attitudes and experiences, and the environment in which they occur.

Questionnaire – an instrument designed and structured to collect data from sample members as required by the research objectives, and which allows for consistent administration resulting in the systematic capture of survey respondents' answers.

Ratio measure – a level of measurement describing a variable with attributes that are rank ordered with exact distances between distances, and a true zero point. Examples of this type of measure include age, number of churches ever attended, and number of times married.

Reliability – refers to whether a particular measurement technique repeatedly applied to a research question yields the same results each time. There are three common ways of testing for reliability: test-retest method, split-half method and using established measures.

Research hypothesis – the hypothesis that suggests that there is a relationship between the variables under study.

Research proposal – a document detailing the research intent, the methodology which will be employed to generate the supportive data, and the total costing of the project.

Sample – a special subset of a population, usually selected for generalizing to the entire population from which it was taken.

Sampling frame – a list of elements in a population from which a sample will be drawn.

Socially desirable response – an answer of questionable accuracy provided by a respondent to an interviewer in the belief that it will be found more satisfying than the truth within the social context.

T-test – a parametric statistical method that shows the extent and direction that a sample mean difference falls from zero on a scale of standard error units.

Table – a concise synopsis of data presented in a structured format comprising title, stub, box head, and body.

Telephone interviewing – a survey data collection method wherein the questionnaire is administered to respondents via telephone.

Theory – a generalized statement which establishes and explains the relationship between a set of specific propositions.

Trace measures – a type of unobtrusive research which involves the study of accretions and erosions.

Univariate analysis – this analysis is concerned with describing a single variable. Data are often presented in the form of means, measures of dispersion and frequency distribution ('uni' refers to one and 'variate' refers to variable).

Unobtrusive research – research which studies human behaviour without affecting it in the process.

Validity – the extent to which an empirical measure actually measures the concept which it purports to measure. While absolute validity can never be proven, social scientists usually assess the validity of a measure by testing for criterion-related validity, content validity and construct validity.

Value – a specific category or a number descriptive of the degree to which the case studied possesses the variable being assessed.

Variable – something which can be measured, can change, and comprises logical groupings of attributes.

Voluntary consent – a research participant's voluntary agreement to participate in a study without fully understanding the purpose or repercussions of involvement.

Bibliography

Annual Statistical Digest 1993/4. Castries: St. Lucia Statistics Department.

Babbie, Earl. 1992. *The Practice of Social Research*. Belmont, CA: Wadsworth Publishing Company.

Bailey, Kenneth. 1989. *The Practice of Social Research*. New York: The Free Press.

Brenner, Michael. 1985. "Survey interviewing". In *The Research Interview*, edited by M. Brenner, J. Brown and D. Canter. London: Academic Press.

Chambers, Claudia M. 1992. "Women at risk? Focus groups comprising low-income women in Jamaica". Report prepared for the University of the West Indies/University of California, Los Angeles. (Restricted.)

Chambers, Claudia M., and Claudia Mitchell-Kernan. 1993. "Transactional sex: AIDS related issues for low-income women in Jamaica". Paper presented at Caribbean Studies Association (CSA) conference. Jamaica.

Chambers, Claudia M., and Clement Branche. 1994a. "Consumer attitudes and behaviours regarding contraceptive methods in Jamaica". Report prepared for the Futures Group/USAID/National Family Planning Board. Jamaica.

Chambers, Claudia M., and Clement Branche. 1994b. "Household food access: a qualitative review of the Jamaican situation". Report prepared for the Caribbean Food and Nutrition Institute/ Planning Institute of Jamaica.

Craib, Ian. 1984. *Modern Social Theory: from Parsons to Habernas*. New York: St Martins.

Dometrius, Nelson. 1992. *Social Statistics Using SPSS*. New York: Harper Collins.

Foddy, W. H. 1988. *Elementary Applied Statistics for Social Sciences*. Sydney: Harper Collins.

Fowler, Floyd. 1988. *Survey Research Methods*. New York: Sage Publishing.

Fowler, Floyd. 1991. "Reducing interviewer-related error through interviewer training, supervision, and other means". In *Measurement Errors in Surveys*, edited by P. Biemer et al. London: John Wiley & Sons.

Fowler, Floyd, and Thomas Mangione. 1990. *Standardized Survey Interviewing: Minimizing Interviewer-related Error*. Newbury Park, CA: Sage Publications.

Gordon, Derek. 1989. "Developing a poverty line for Jamaica: identifying the poor". Planning Institute of Jamaica. Working Paper No. 3.

Gravetter, Frederick J. 1988. *Statistics for the Behavioural Sciences*. San Francisco: West Publishing Company.

Greenbaum, Thomas. 1988. *The Practical Handbook and Guide to Focus Group Research*. Lexington, MA.: Lexington Books.

Guilford, J. P. 1965. *Fundamental Statistics in Psychology and Education*. New York: McGraw-Hill.

Hollis, F. 1964. *Casework: a Psychosocial Therapy*. New York: London House.

Hughes, Everett C. 1958. *Men and their Work*. New York: The Free Press.

Levin, Jack, and James A. Fox. 1994. *Elementary Statistics in Social Research*. New York: Harper Collins College Publishers.

Manley, Rachel. 1989. *Edna Manley: the Diaries*. Kingston Jamaica: Heinemann Publishers (Caribbean).

Mehan, Hugh, and Houstan Wood. 1994. "Five features of reality". In *The Production of Reality: Essays and Readings in Social Psychology*, edited by Peter Kollock and Jodi O'Brien. Newbury Park, CA: Pine Forge Press.

Moser, C. A., and G. Kalton. 1986. *Survey Methods in Social Investigation*. Brookfield, VT: Gower Publishing Company.

Morgan, David. 1988. *Focus Groups as Qualitative Research*. Newbury Park, CA: Sage Publications.

Myrdal, Gunnar. 1968. *The Asian Drama: an Enquiry into the Poverty of Nations*. New York: Pantheon Press.

Newman, Lawrence. 1991. *Social Research Methods*. Needham Heights, MA: Allyn and Bacon.

Oppenheim. A. N. 1992. *Questionnaire Design, Interviewing and Attitude Measurement*. London: Printer Publishers.

The Oxford Reference Dictionary. 1989. Oxford: Clarendon Press.

Population and Housing Census. 1991. Commonwealth of Dominica.

Sarantakos, S. 1993. *Social Research*. London: Macmillan Press.

Schuman, Howard, and Stanley Presser. 1981. *Questions and Answers in Attitude Surveys*. SAn Diego: Academic Press.

Scrimshaw, Nevin, and Gary Gleason (eds). 1992. *Rapid Assessment Procedures: Qualitative Methodologies for Planning and Evaluation of Health-related Programmes*. Boston: International Nutrition Foundation for Developing Countries.

Shaughnessy, John J., and Eugene B. Zechmeister. 1994. *Research Methods in Psychology*. New York: McGraw-Hill.

Statistical Review. 1993. Kingston: Jamaica Public Service Co.

Tuckman, Bruce. 1978. *Conducting Educational Research*. San Diego: Harcourt Brace Jovanovitch.

USA. 1980. *National Association of Social Workers Code of Ethics*.

USA. 1995. *Code of Ethics of the American Sociological Association*.

Veto, Gennaro F., and Edward J. Latessa, 1989. *Statistical Applications in Criminal Justice*. London: Sage Publications.

Webb, E. J., D. T. Campbell, R. D. Schwartz, L. Sechrest, and J. B. Grove. 1949. *Nonreactive Measures in the Social Sciences*. Boston: Houghton Mifflin.

Webb, Eugene J., Donald T. Campbell, Richard D. Schwartz, and Lee Sechrest. 1966. *Unobtrusive Measures: Nonreactive Research in the Social Sciences*. Chicago: Rand McNally. Quoted in K. Bailey, *Methods of Social Research* (London: The Free Press 1987).

Wint, E. "The consequences of infertility: a focus on self-concept measurement in social work practice". PhD diss., University of the West Indies.

Wint, E., and Janet Brown. "Promoting effective parenting". *Child Welfare*. Vol. 66 no. 6 (1987): 507–16.